# Think RE! 1

Michael Brewer • Gary Green • Verity Lush

Ruth Mantin • Alison Philips • Peter Smith

Series editor: Janet Dyson  Consultant: Pamela Draycott

D0183364

**www.heinemann.co.uk**
✓ Free online support
✓ Useful weblinks
✓ 24 hour online ordering

**01865 888058**

**Heinemann**
*Inspiring generations*

Heinemann is an imprint of Pearson Education Limited, a company incorporated in England and Wales, having its registered office at Edinburgh Gate, Harlow, Essex, CM20 2JE. Registered company number: 872828

Heinemann is a registered trademark of Pearson Education Limited

© Harcourt Education Limited, 2005

First published 2005

11
10

British Library Cataloguing in Publication Data is available from the British Library on request.

ISBN: 978 0 435307 17 2

Produced by Bridge Creative Services Ltd

Original illustrations © Harcourt Education Limited, 2005
Illustrated by Jane Smith and Andrew Skilleter

Printed and bound in China (CTPS/10)

Cover photo: © Green flower with rings of green petals © Corbis

Picture research by Virginia Stroud-Lewis

**Acknowledgements**
Every effort has been made to contact copyright holders of material reproduced in this book. Any omissions will be rectified in subsequent printings if notice is given to the publishers.

**Faith readers**
Thanks to the following for their help and advice on all religious content:

Jonathan Brandman          Board of Deputies of British Jews
Rasamandala Das            Oxford Centre for Vishnu Hindu Studies
Dick Powell                 Culham Institue
Anil Goonewardene          Buddhist Society

**Copyright**
Thanks to Renault and Thierry Henry for the still from the televison advert 'Va Va Voom', page 80 : © Renault and Thierry Henry; Love is...cartoon, page 84 : © Bill Asprey. Reproduced with kind permission.

All Bible passages have been taken from the New International Version.

**Photo acknowledgements**
The publishers would like to thank the following for permission to use photographs:
AKG-Images/British Museum p. 26; Alamy Images/Christine Osborne/World Religions Library p. 35; Alamy Images/Photofusion p. 47; Alamy Images/Stock Connection Distribution /Peter Bisset p. 69; AP Photo/L'Osservatore Romano p. 78 (left); Art Directors and Trip p. 53; p. 55; Art Directors and Trip/Itzhak Genut p. 106; Art Directors and Trip/Esther James p. 49; Art Directors and Trip/Helene Rogers p. 48; p. 52; p. 54; p. 65; p. 87; Bridgeman Art Library/Biblioteca Reale, Turin, Italy, Alinari p. 62; Bridgeman Art Library/Hospital Tavera, Toledo, Spain p. 45 (bottom); Bridgeman Art Library/Private Collection p. 60; Bridgeman Art Library/ Vatican Museums and Galleries, Vatican City, Italy/www.bridgeman.co.uk p. 45 (top); Bridgeman Art Library/© Whitworth Art Gallery, The University of Manchester, UK/ www.bridgeman.co.uk p. 42; Circa Photo Library p. 36; p. 78 (centre); p. 86; Corbis p. 10 (bottom right); p. 34; p. 102; Corbis/ Dave Bartruff p. 10 (bottom left); p. 13; Corbis/Bettmann p. 33 (right); p. 82; Corbis/Barnabas Bosshart p. 32; Corbis/Keith Dannemiller p. 107; Corbis/Digital Art p. 59; p. 60 (top); p. 72; Corbis/Marcel Hartmann p. 99; Corbis/ Andrew Holbrooke p. 17; Corbis/Karen Huntt p. 94; Corbis/Brooks Kraft p. 76; Corbis/Chris Lisle p. 85; Corbis/Alen MacWeeney p. 23; p. 38; Corbis/Gideon Mendel p. 10 (bottom centre); Corbis/ Christine Osborne p. 78 (right); Corbis/Ricki Rosen p. 41; p. 56; Corbis/Alan Schein Photography p. 95; Corbis/Liba Taylor p. 64; Corbis/Arthur Thévenart p. 33 (centre); Corbis/Penny Tweedie p. 27; EPA/European Press Agency/EPA/EMPICS p. 10 (top); Getty Images/PhotoDisc p. 5; p. 14; Kobal Collection/Universal/Ralph Nelson Jr p. 44; Mary Evans Picture Library/Harry Price Collection p. 96; PA/Empics/Natural History Museum p. 104; Rex p. 43; Robert Harding World Imagery p. 51; Sovfoto p. 105; Ginny Stroud-Lewis p. 100.

# CONTENTS

# CHAPTER 1

# WHAT IS BELIEF?

## THE BIGGER PICTURE

In this chapter you will find out what belief is and what it means to some people to have religious beliefs. You will also explore the link between belief and faith.

### WHAT?

You will:
- analyse the difference between a belief, a fact and an opinion
- find out what religious belief and faith are
- investigate the beliefs of different religions
- explore how religious beliefs affect people's actions
- evaluate the rewards and difficulties involved in having belief
- reflect on your own beliefs.

### HOW?

By:
- identifying beliefs, opinions and facts
- considering how specific people have put their faith into practice
- reflecting on how religious believers would behave in different situations
- judging for yourself what it means to have a religious belief.

### WHY?

Because:
- more than three quarters of the world's population follow a religion
- our beliefs influence how we act, so to understand people we need to understand their beliefs
- what we believe can affect how we live and our opinions.

## KEY IDEAS

- A belief is a statement that you think is true but you cannot prove.
- To believe means to have faith or trust in something.
- Some people might believe in a variety of things but might not act on these beliefs, for example some people might believe that God exists but not worship God.
- Believing in something means you have to put your trust in something.

## KEY WORDS

| | |
|---|---|
| Belief | Faith |
| Soul | Spirit |
| Sacred | Holy |
| Shahadah | Sawm |
| Zakah | Nirvana |
| Meditation | Five Precepts |

In this lesson you will:
- investigate how religion has an effect on our lives
- understand why RE is studied in school
- discover what you know about the world's religions.

**R**eligious education (RE) is all about finding out what people believe, how they behave and what they think is important. It explores how different people search for and find meaning in their lives. In RE, you will not only learn about other people, you will also be asked to think about yourself and your own beliefs and opinions.

**?**

## THINK ABOUT IT!

1. Copy out the table below. Sort the information and symbols into the correct places.

| Religion | Buddhism | Christianity | Hinduism | Islam | Judaism | Sikhism |
|---|---|---|---|---|---|---|
| **Founder/ leader** | | | | | | |
| **Symbol** | | | | | | |
| **Sacred writings** | | | | | | |
| **Place of worship** | | | | | | |
| **Festivals** | | | | | | |

- **People:** Abraham, the Buddha, Guru Nanak, Jesus, Muhammmad, unknown.
- **Symbols:**

- **Sacred writings:** Bible, Dhammapada, Guru Granth Sahib, Mahabharata, Qur'an, Torah, Tripitaka, Vedas.
- **Places of worship:** church, gurdwara, mandir, mosque, shrine/temple, synagogue.
- **Festivals:** Baisakhi, Christmas, Divali, Easter, gurpurb, Hannukah, Holi, Id-ul-Adha, Id-ul-Fitr, Obon, Passover, Pentecost/Whitsun, Wesak, Yom Kippur.

## ● **WHY DO WE STUDY RE?**

We all have beliefs: beliefs about what is right and wrong, how we should treat others, why we are here.

Here are some reasons teenagers have given as an answer to the question, 'Why do we study RE?'

Why do we study RE?

**A)** Over three quarters of the world say that they follow a religion, so this makes religion an important influence on people's lives.

**B)** If we want to understand our world, we need to understand the people around us.

**C)** You only need to watch the news to understand how important it is to understand other people's religion. If people did this, there would be less violence in the world.

**F)** Some of the people who have inspired others the most and changed the world have been religious. Think of people like Gandhi and Mother Teresa.

**D)** RE has made me a much more tolerant person. I have learnt how to listen to others and consider viewpoints that are different to my own.

**G)** RE teaches me to think about the important questions in life like 'why am I here?' 'why is there suffering and evil?' and 'what happens when I die?'

**E)** RE helps me understand myself. It is about forming my own ideas and opinions on what I believe about important moral issues such as abortion, euthanasia, war, poverty, crime and punishment.

**H)** RE teaches me to think about the values religions hold. Ideas such as forgiveness, justice and fairness for all people, concern for our world and the environment seem important to me.

### **THINK ABOUT IT!**

2. Read the statements in speech bubbles A–H. Which of these do you think are the most important reasons for studying RE? Explain your answer. What else can you add?

3. Religion can influence people's lives. In what ways can your actions influence others?

4. Design a poster that shows why you think it is important to study RE in school. Include:
   - the reasons for studying RE
   - some of the aspects and religions covered
   - important questions that might be asked or answered.

# 1.2 WHAT IS BELIEF?

In this lesson you will:
- understand what **belief** means
- explore the difference between a belief, a fact and an opinion
- make connections between belief and **faith**.

## WHAT IS BELIEF?

In order to understand what belief is, you need to know the difference between a belief, a fact and an opinion.

### THINK ABOUT IT!

1. Read the following statements and decide which is a belief, which is a fact and which is an opinion. Give reasons for your answers.
   a) Arsenal is the best football team.
   b) The United Kingdom has a prime minister.
   c) Chewing gum helps you to concentrate.
   d) The Qur'an is the Muslim holy book.
   e) Flowers are beautiful.
   f) People cannot travel faster than the speed of light.
   g) It is wrong to murder.
   h) The Eightfold Path of Buddhism is a pattern for living.
   i) The universe exists.
   j) Prayer can make things happen.

## SOME SIMPLE DEFINITIONS

- A belief is a statement you think is true but you cannot prove. For example, 'I believe that God exists.'
- An opinion is your own personal view on a subject. For example, 'In my opinion, cats make better pets than dogs.'
- A fact is something you can prove to be true. For example, 'I know that Paris is the capital of France.'

We sometimes use language so vaguely that we might often say 'I believe ...' when we really mean 'I think ...'

For example, when Zak says, 'I believe it is wrong to kill animals for food,' he might really mean, 'In my opinion it is wrong to kill animals for food.' He is expressing his own opinion.

### THINK ABOUT IT!

2. Look back at your answers to Think about it! 1. Now that you know the definitions would you change any of your answers? Why?

## THINK ABOUT IT!

**3.** Do you agree with where these statements have been placed? Do you think any can be moved or rewritten? Why/why not?

**Belief**
a) I believe that God wants me to follow the laws of the land.
b) I believe that my football team will win tomorrow.

**Opinion**
c) I think everyone should be vegetarian because it is wrong to kill animals for food.
d) I think we should be allowed to wear what we like to school.

**Fact**
e) I know that I love God.
f) 3 + 3 = 6.

## ● WHAT IS FAITH?

Charles Blondin was a man who believed in himself. He was a famous tightrope walker. In 1859, a huge crowd watched as he walked across Niagara Falls on a tightrope 1100 feet (335 metres) long. He then made the return journey pushing a wheelbarrow. His manager climbed into the wheelbarrow and they crossed once more.

Blondin asked the crowd whether they believed he could do it again. They were confident that he could. So he said, 'Well, get in then and I'll take you across.'

Everyone refused. They all failed to trust him.

Faith requires belief *and* trust. Look back again at the definition of belief on these pages. When people are not able to prove that something exists, they need to trust that it is there.

## THINK ABOUT IT!

**4.** What does it mean to have faith in someone?

**5.** Make a list of the people you trust and believe in. Against each name, make a note of why you believe and trust in that person.

**6. a)** Is it important to believe in people and trust them? Explain your answer.
**b)** Are there any dangers in believing and trusting in people? Give reasons for your answer.

In this lesson you will:
● analyse what being religious means
● reflect on how beliefs can be expressed in actions
● evaluate what difference having a religious belief might make to someone's life.

**M**any people in the world today say that they are religious. But what exactly does this mean?

**?**

### THINK ABOUT IT!

**1. a)** What do you think makes a person religious? In pairs, make a list of your ideas.

**b)** Now compare your ideas with another pair. How are they similar? How are they different?

**2.** Look at the pictures on this page. Which do you think are religious? Give reasons for your choices.

When you thought about what makes a person religious, did you include any of the following?

### ● Belief in a spiritual dimension to life

Many people believe that there is more to a human being than the physical body. They believe that there is an inner self that cannot be broken down into elements. It is a bit like electricity – you cannot see it, but you know it is there.

Many religious people believe in life after death and some also believe that people have a **soul** or a **spirit**.

### KEY WORDS

**Soul** the non-physical, spiritual or emotional centre of a person that is said to survive death

**Spirit** the inner part of a person, often connected to feelings

**Sacred** dedicated to a God or religious purpose

Lots of religious people also believe that there is a creator, God or an 'ultimate truth' behind this world, guiding and directing it.

### ● Belief that life is *sacred*

Most followers of religion believe that life is sacred. This means they believe that all life, including animals, should be treated with respect. For some people, this will mean thinking carefully about how they treat all life.

### ● Belief that life has a meaning

Many religious people believe that life has a purpose. Following a religion helps them to make sense of their life. It helps them to deal with big questions such as 'why are we here?' and 'why is there suffering in the world?'

Some religious people believe that their purpose in life is to serve God and others . Others believe that they will be continually reborn into other lives until they have lived a life which is good enough to earn them heavenly bliss.

## ● HOW DO BELIEFS AFFECT ACTIONS?

What people believe is often seen in the way they behave and the way they treat the people around them. For example, they might stand up for human rights, speak out against oppression, look after the poor or do charity work. Expressing their beliefs in actions often involves putting others before themselves and making sacrifices.

Holding religious beliefs can also affect someone's day-to-day life. Many religions have rules. These can cover all sorts of things, for example:

● what to wear

● what to eat

● how to worship and pray

● celebrations and festivals.

## ● PRAYER AND MEDITATION

A religious person who believes in God might want to find time to pray. They will pray for different reasons:

● to communicate with God

● to seek God's guidance

● to praise and worship God

● to pray for others.

Some religious people meditate in order to think deeply about something or to calm their minds in order to develop understanding.

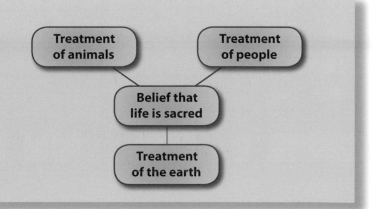

In this lesson you will:
- investigate what Christians believe about Jesus
- identify some of your own beliefs and how these influence you
- evaluate the relevance of the teachings of Jesus in the world today.

Christianity is the world's largest religion. It has over two billion followers. But why has Jesus had such an impact on so many people? Do his teachings really make a difference to people's lives today?

## WHAT DO CHRISTIANS BELIEVE ABOUT JESUS?

Read each of the speech bubbles below to find out what some Christians believe about Jesus. Then read the quotations A–E to find out what the Bible says about Jesus.

**1** I believe that Jesus was God in human form. This belief is called 'incarnation'. Jesus was born into poverty as a carpenter's son.

**2** 'Jesus' means 'God saves'. I believe that Jesus saved humans from sin by dying on the cross.

**3** I believe that Jesus was a revolutionary who turned the world upside down. He challenged people to completely rethink their attitudes and change their lives.

**4** I believe that Jesus is God's way of showing humans what love is. In the wedding service in my church, the priest always asks the couple if they are willing to do the best for each other no matter what it might cost them. This is the kind of love I believe God shows through Jesus and wants people to show to one another.

**5** I believe that Jesus knows who I am and is my best friend. Jesus was betrayed, rejected, and his best friend said he did not know him. There is nothing I can go through that he has not been through.

### THINK ABOUT IT!

**1.** What do you know about Jesus? Write a few sentences to express your thoughts on who Jesus was.

**2.** Read the Bible quotes (A-E) on page 13. Now match each speech bubble to the relevant quotes.

**3. a)** What beliefs do you hold? How do your beliefs affect your life? Do any of these beliefs cause you problems or difficulities?

**b)** Choose one of the speech bubbles. How might this belief influence the way someone lives their life? What difficulties might that person might experience if they live by their beliefs?

**A**

'The one I kiss is the man: arrest him.'

*Matthew 26: 45–9, 69–75*

**B**

'She [Mary] wrapped him [Jesus] in cloths and placed him in a manger, because there was no room for them in the inn.'

*Luke 2: 7*

**C**

'Carrying his own cross, he went out to the place of the Skull (which in Aramaic is called Golgotha). Here they crucified him ...'

*John 19: 17–18*

**D**

'Love the Lord your God with all your heart and with all your soul and with all your mind ... Love your neighbour as yourself.'

*Mark 12: 30, 33*

**E**

'No servant is greater than his master, nor is a messenger greater than the one who sent him.'

*John 13: 16*

## ● HOW DO CHRISTIANS PUT THESE BELIEFS INTO PRACTICE IN THEIR LIVES?

Corrie ten Boom and her sister Betsie were part of a Christian family living in the Netherlands in the 1930s. As Hitler and the Nazi Party increased their power, Corrie's family became more aware that the Jews were being persecuted. Jews disappeared overnight, their shops and synagogues were destroyed and they were forced to wear a yellow Star of David, a symbol of Judaism.

Corrie's family decided to help the Jews and they became part of an underground movement. They hid Jews in a secret room in their home.

The Nazis eventually arrested Corrie and her family. They were questioned about their activities and were imprisoned.

Corrie and Betsie were taken to Ravensbruck concentration camp where they taught their fellow prisoners about God's love. They prayed not just for their fellow prisoners but also for the German guards.

Corrie's father and Betsie both died while in prison. However, Corrie herself was released from Ravensbruck on 31 December 1944.

⌒ **This hole in the brick wall is the hiding place in Corrie ten Boom's house in Haarlem.**

### THINK ABOUT IT!

4. Which of the teachings (from the Bible) above do you think Corrie demonstrated? Give reasons for your answer.

5. Create a presentation to help people understand the importance of Jesus' teachings for Christians. Remember to think about the following in your presentation:
   ● what his teachings are about
   ● how you think the world would improve if people followed the Christian teachings
   ● what might be involved in following the Christian teachings.

In this lesson you will:
- investigate what Muslims believe about Allah
- explain how these beliefs in Allah affect Muslims' actions
- express your own beliefs and explain how you put them into action

## BELIEF IN ALLAH

'There is no God but Allah, Muhammad is the messenger of Allah.'

This statement is called the **Shahadah**. It is a declaration of faith in Allah and sums up what Muslims believe.

Muslims believe that Islam is a complete way of life given to them by Allah. The word 'Islam' means 'to submit' or 'surrender'. A Muslim is one who submits to the will of Allah.

Muslims believe that Muhammad is Allah's messenger and that Allah revealed the Qur'an to Muhammad. They do not believe that Muhammad started Islam.

Muslim beliefs can be broken down into three parts.

1 Tawhid – the oneness of Allah
   - Belief in Allah
   - Belief in the will of Allah

2 Risalah – the role of the prophets
   - Belief in Allah's angels
   - Belief in Allah's books
   - Belief in Allah's prophets

3 Akhirah – life after death
   - Belief in life after death
   - Belief in the Day of Judgement

On page 15, Sabeel explains what these beliefs mean to him.

◗ **The use of images of God or of the human form is forbidden in Islam so all decorations are calligraphy and geometric designs. How does the design of the windows in this picture symbolise Muslim beliefs about God?**

## ● TAWHID

'As a Muslim, I believe that Allah is the creator who knows everything, sees everything and can do anything. Allah is eternal and nothing can be compared to Him.

'I also believe that everything that happens is according to Allah's will. He is in charge, but I have the choice to do good or evil. You might hear a Muslim saying "Insh'Allah". This means "if God wills it". It shows that we accept and submit to Allah who knows what is best.'

Sabeel

## ● RISALAH

'Allah has sent His angels or messengers of light. The angels do Allah's will and carry His messages to the prophets. They are present at all times but are invisible unless revealed in a human or awesome form.

'Allah has revealed His guidance to the prophets. There are 25 prophets, starting with Adam and finishing with Muhammad.' Allah's guidance is written down in **holy** books. Because some of these books were lost or altered, Allah revealed the Qur'an to Muhammad as His last and final message to humans.'

Sabeel

## ● AKHIRAH

'I believe that life has two parts. First there is a brief stay on earth. This is to test whether we turn towards Allah or turn away from Him. This is followed by eternal life. Eternal life is more important because it lasts forever.

'On the Day of Judgement, Allah will judge everyone on their deeds and their faith. Believers will be rewarded and will enter paradise. Unbelievers will go to hell.'

Sabeel

## ? THINK ABOUT IT!

1. What idea of Allah do you get from reading this information? Write a couple of sentences showing your thoughts under each heading: Tawhid, Risalah, Akhirah.

2. Copy and complete the following table to show how these beliefs will affect the way a Muslim lives his or her life. Think about things he or she might do and the way in which he or she might behave.

| Belief | Ways that this belief will affect a Muslim's life |
|---|---|
| Belief in Allah and in the will of Allah | |
| Muslims will not make a picture or statue of Allah because nothing can be compared to Allah. | |
| Belief in Allah's angels, books and prophets | |
| Belief in life after death and the Day of Judgement | |

In this lesson you will:
- explore what the Five Pillars of Islam are
- reflect on how two of the Five Pillars of Islam affect a Muslim's life
- express your own response to the concept of zakah
- reflect on your own response to helping people in need.

## THE FIVE PILLARS OF ISLAM

An important part of Muslim life is worshipping Allah. Worship is divided into five duties called the Five Pillars of Islam. The illustration below shows how the Muslim beliefs in Allah form the foundation stones of Islam. They are connected to the Five Pillars of Islam, which are the support for a Muslim's life. In this lesson we will find out about two of the five pillars; **Sawm** and **Zakah**.

| SHAHADAH Declaration of faith | | SALAH Prayer five times a day | | ZAKAH Giving 2.5 per cent, or one fortieth, of savings to those in need | | SAWM Fasting during daylight hours during Ramadan | | HAJJ Pilgamage to Makkah once in a lifetime | |
|---|---|---|---|---|---|---|---|---|---|
| Belief in Allah | Belief in the will of Allah | Belief in Allah's angels | Belief in Allah's books | Belief in Allah's prophets | | Belief in life after death | | Belief in the Day of Judgement | |

**?**

### THINK ABOUT IT!

1. In what ways do you think that prayer at five set times a day might help someone be a better Muslim?

## SAWM

**Sawm** means fasting, going without food during daylight hours for the month of Ramadan. During Ramadan, Muslims remember how Muhammad received his first revelation of the Qur'an from Allah.

Sawm is also important because Muhammad practised it.

Fasting helps Muslims learn about what it is like to be hungry. They can also understand the needs of the poor in developing countries. They learn to appreciate the good things Allah has given them instead of taking them for granted. Above all, they learn how to overcome greed and selfishness and control their body by strengthening their will power.

'O you who believe. Fasting is ordered for you, as it was ordered for those before you so that you may learn self-discipline and ward off evil.'

*Surah 2: 183*

## THINK ABOUT IT!

2. Make a list of the reasons why Muslims fast. Which do you think is the most important reason? Explain your answer.

3. Imagine that you are a Muslim who has just fasted. Write a diary after your fast, recording:
   - how fasting has changed the way you see life
   - what actions would you now like to take to improve yourself and help others.

**KEY WORDS**

**Sawm** Islamic practice of fasting from sunrise to sunset

**Zakah** Islamic practice of giving 2.5 per cent of savings to those in need

## ● ZAKAH

Muslims believe that Allah has given everything to them. This includes their gifts and talents, their money and their possessions. They also believe that when they die they will be held accountable for how they have used all these things.

Muslims will often give freely to those in need. This type of giving is called sadaqah.

**Zakah**, however, is a duty and is like a form of tax. All Muslims worldwide who have a certain amount of wealth must give a percentage of their savings to help the poor and the needy. Zakah is paid once every year.

The word 'zakah' means to 'purify' or 'cleanse.' Muslims believe that in giving zakah they are cleansing themselves from greed and selfishness.

⊃ **How does this make you feel? What practical things could a Muslim do in order to change this situation?**

## THINK ABOUT IT!

4. What do Muslims mean when they say:
   - zakah is an act of worship
   - zakah is a way of purifying your wealth
   - zakah is a test?

5. Why do you think Muslims are required to pay a percentage of their savings rather than their income?

6. 'What I do with my money is my business.' How would you personally respond to this statement? What do you think a Muslim would say in reply to this statement?

In this lesson you will:
- find out about some Buddhist beliefs
- investigate how these beliefs are reflected in the Noble Eightfold Path and the Five Precepts
- evaluate which beliefs you think are most important.

## ● WHO WAS THE BUDDHA?

Prince Siddhartha was born into a life of luxury. His father gave him everything he wanted, but he also tried to protect his son from pain and suffering. This was because at Siddhartha's birth, six wise men had told his father his son would become a great king. A wise man called Asita said he would become a Buddha.

Despite the pleasures and wealth that surrounded him, Siddhartha was unhappy and restless. He eventually persuaded his charioteer to take him into the city. There he saw an old man, a sick man and a dead man. Siddhartha was shocked by the realities of life and the suffering he saw.

He then saw a homeless holy man and realized he was happy, peaceful and fulfilled. As a result, Siddhartha gave up his life in the palace and set out to find the answer to the questions that he had been asking.

After six years of searching, Siddhartha **meditated** under the Bodhi Tree (the tree of wisdom). Here he found Enlightenment: he woke up to the truth and became a Buddha – the Enlightened one.

The Buddha taught that one way to achieve Enlightenment (**Nirvana**) and to avoid desire was to follow the Noble Eightfold Path. The Noble Eightfold Path includes some of the central beliefs of Buddhism.

### THINK ABOUT IT!

1. What questions do you think Siddhartha was asking himself?

### KEY WORDS

**Meditation** calming the mind by concentrating

**Nirvana** point at which Enlightenment has been achieved

**Five Precepts** five moral intentions that Buddhists try to live their life by

# ● THE NOBLE EIGHTFOLD PATH

### ● Step 1 – right vision

Buddhists must accept that life involves pain and suffering. They must also realize that suffering can be overcome by following the Noble Eightfold Path.

### ● Step 2 – right intention

Buddhists must try to overcome temptation. They should be kind to all living things and should try not to become angry. They should keep a peaceful mind.

### ● Step 3 – right speech

Buddhists must always speak in a way that shows respect to others. This means they should not tell lies, be deceitful or gossip.

### ● Step 4 – right action

Buddhists should live according to the **Five Precepts**. The Five Precepts are as follows.

**1**  Avoid taking life and harming living things.
**2**  Avoid taking what is not given (do not steal).
**3**  Avoid any harmful sexual activity.
**4**  Avoid speaking falsely (do not lie or gossip).
**5**  Avoid drink and drugs that can cloud the mind.

### ● Step 5 – right livelihood

Buddhists should earn their living in an honest, legal and peaceful way. The Buddha listed four activities that harm others and which should be avoided.

**1**  Dealing in weapons, for example selling or using guns.
**2**  Dealing in human beings, for example slavery.
**3**  Dealing in flesh, for example raising animals for slaughter, butchery, fishing.
**4**  Dealing alcohol, tobacco and illegal drugs.

### ● Step 6 – right effort

Buddhists must turn away from bad thoughts and must work hard to do good and develop good thoughts.

### ● Step 7 – right awareness

Buddhists must develop full control of their thoughts, speech and actions. They need to realize that their actions will have consequences. However, they must also make the most of the present moment.

### ● Step 8 – right concentration

Buddhists must aim to be free from worry and envy. Meditation helps to achieve this calm and peace. It also helps Buddhists to know their inner selves and see themselves more clearly.

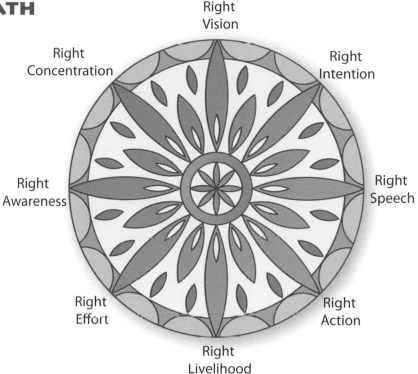

Right Vision
Right Concentration
Right Intention
Right Awareness
Right Speech
Right Effort
Right Action
Right Livelihood

**The symbol of the Noble Eightfold Path is a wheel with eight spokes. The wheel helps to remind Buddhists of the circle of life.**

## **THINK ABOUT IT!**

**2.** Why do you think that Buddhists believe they should not harm living things? Discuss your answer with a partner.

**3.** Rank the Five Precepts in the order you consider to be most important. Explain your choice.

**4.** Which of the steps on the Noble Eightfold Path would you find most difficult and why?

**5.** In what ways would you have to change if you were following the Noble Eightfold Path?

## WHAT THE TASK IS ALL ABOUT:

**1 a)** You have sent an email to a Buddhist and either a Christian or a Muslim, asking them what their religion teaches about the right way to behave and act in life. Write their replies to your email.

> Dear Sir or Madam,
>
> I am carrying out a survey of people's religious beliefs and wondered if you could help me by answering the questions below.
>
> 1 What does your religion teach you about how to treat other people?
>
> 2 What does your religion teach you about how to treat animals and the world around us?
>
> 3 What do you think is the most important belief and why?
>
> 4 How has following your religion changed you as a person?
>
> 5 If you had to choose three words to express what is important in your religion, what would they be?

**b)** Write a short paragraph to explain the similarities and differences between the two religions' answers.

**2 a)** From the religions you have studied, which three beliefs do you think are:

- the most important for our world today?
- the most important ones for you personally to live by? Why?

**b)** If you had to choose to live by the teachings of one of the religions you have studied, which would you choose and why? If none, explain why not.

## WHAT YOU NEED TO DO TO COMPLETE THE TASK:

**1** In each reply you need to explain:

- why the teaching is important
- what differences following this teaching will make
- why someone would want to follow the teaching and what they hope will happen if they follow it
- the difference it makes to their lives and how it will change them.

**2** Make sure you explain why you have chosen the three beliefs. Show clearly how they benefit the world and what happens when they are not present/practised.

## HINTS AND TIPS

**1** Think about situations that will illustrate some of the important beliefs, for example forgiveness in Christianity or right intention/speech in Buddhism. Try to explain why the decision might be hard. Make sure the member of the religion explains both sides of the argument.

**2** Make sure that you explain your answers and reasons fully, and try to give a variety of reasons to support your viewpoints. Make sure you give clear examples and illustrations.

| TO ACHIEVE | YOU WILL NEED TO |
|---|---|
| Level 3 | Describe some of the beliefs and teachings of the religions you have studied and show how they influence people's lives. |
| Level 4 | Show that you understand why the members of the religions follow the beliefs and teachings. Explain the reasons they might respond in this way and also how you might respond. Support your answers with clear reasons. |
| Level 5 | Explain what difference following the teachings might make to a believer's life and identify some similarities and differences between them. Explain the beliefs that lead them to behave in this way. Consider beliefs thoughtfully and relate them clearly to your own life and others' lives. |
| Level 6 | Compare the two religions' beliefs and explain the similarities and differences. Explain clearly the significance of their beliefs and show how they are expressed in a variety of ways. Evaluate the beliefs, relating them to your own and others' lives, and support your answers with thoughtful reasons. Show an appreciation of the significance of these teachings. |

# CODE BREAKING

## THE BIGGER PICTURE

In this chapter you will examine the ways in which religions express their beliefs through **symbols** and stories. Very often these symbols and stories may seem strange to people outside the religion. You are going to see that understanding religious language and practice is like breaking a code.

### WHAT?

You will:

- examine the ways in which religions and worldviews use symbols and stories to express their ideas
- analyse and explain the importance of understanding symbolic images, language and action
- reflect on the different ways that people use symbols and stories to make sense of the world.

### HOW?

By:

- looking carefully at symbols, stories, images and actions
- learning how to 'decode' the symbols and stories
- rethinking your ideas about what makes something 'true'
- showing that you can interpret symbolic images and language.

### WHY?

Because:

- in order to understand other people, you need to know the ideas that are important to them
- to do this, you need to be able to interpret or 'decode' the ways that people use language and symbols to express their beliefs
- this will help you make sense of the world around you and realize that there are many opinions about what makes something 'true'.

## KEY IDEAS

- Religious and non-religious symbols are in daily use all around the world.
- You use symbolic language and actions everyday, but you may not even realize it!
- Your own symbols probably just seem 'normal'. To someone else, however, they might appear strange or confusing.
- Symbols can be used and interpreted differently.
- If you are going to understand other people, you need to understand the symbols they use.

☾ 'Mandala' is an ancient word for 'circle'. They are colourful designs that show symbols in a symmetrical pattern. People from many religions use mandalas to help them concentrate in order to pray or meditate. Some mandala patterns are thousands of years old, but modern artists are also creating new ones.

## KEY WORDS

| | |
|---|---|
| Symbols | Qur'an |
| Symmetrical | Hadith |
| Meditate | Trimurti |
| Cultures | Brahman |
| Epic | Allah |
| Aboriginal | Calligraphy |
| Dreamtime | Ahimsa |
| Deities | Shahadah |
| Scholars | Rituals |
| Narrative | Puja |
| Gospel | Murti |
| Myth | |

In this lesson you will:

- evaluate the idea that symbols are an important method of communication
- understand that symbols need to be interpreted carefully
- reflect upon how symbols are used to convey ideas, beliefs and feelings.

**M**any of us use and understand different codes every day, often without really thinking about it. Codes can be an effective way to communicate ideas, instructions and beliefs.

## THINK ABOUT IT!

**1.** This is a key word written in code: *hbnylo.* Try breaking the code using the alphabet as it is written below.

| A | B | C | D | E | F | G | H | I | J | K | L | M | N | O | P | Q | R | S | T | U | V | W | X | Y | Z |
|---|---|---|---|---|---|---|---|---|---|---|---|---|---|---|---|---|---|---|---|---|---|---|---|---|---|
| Z | Y | X | W | V | U | T | S | R | Q | P | O | N | M | L | K | J | I | H | G | F | E | D | C | B | A |

Understanding how to use this code will make it possible to work out what the key word is. However, codes can seem meaningless unless you know how to interpret them.

This is often a problem that we face when we try to understand the ideas, beliefs and practices of others, especially when it comes to religion. It is quite common for religious ideas and beliefs to be expressed through the use of symbols. These symbols can be actions, images, objects or stories. Like a code, they can be confusing if we do not know how to read them.

In this lesson, you will examine different ways that symbols are used and understood. It is important to remember that different individuals or groups can understand the same symbol very differently. There will not necessarily be a right or wrong way to understand a symbol.

## ● WHAT IS A SYMBOL?

The simplest definition of a **symbol** is 'language, objects, images or actions that represent something other than themselves'. For example, the visual image of a dove is often used to represent the idea of peace, rather than anything to do with a species of bird.

Although symbols can be difficult to understand, they perform an essential part of the way that we communicate with one another. Even with hundreds of thousands of words in the English language alone, we still sometimes find it very difficult to express our ideas, beliefs and feelings fully. Sometimes, symbols are a much better way to communicate because they allow for a range of possible meanings to be discussed.

## **THINK ABOUT IT!**

2.  At some point, we are all lost for words.
    a)  Think of an idea, belief or feeling that you sometimes find hard to explain. Examples might include anger, love, and life after death.
    b)  Design a symbol to illustrate your idea, belief or feeling. Include an explanation of your choice and design. Remember that each person's experiences and expressions of life are different.

# ● **WONDERFUL WATER!**

One symbol that is used by many religions is water. Although water is used in different ways, it is always understood for its importance to life and the fact that while we cannot live without it, it can easily become a deadly force.

Below are two accounts of how water is used symbolically within different religions.

**KEY WORDS**

**Symbol** something which is used to represent something else

In the Roman Catholic Church, water is used as a common symbol throughout a person's life. As an infant, I was baptized. Water was sprinkled over me to symbolize being cleansed of sin and being brought into a new life in the Church. At my grandmother's funeral, the priest sprinkled holy water on the coffin to remind us of her baptism and that through baptism we are given eternal life with God.

**Kim**

As a Muslim, water has a central role in my daily worship. Before prayer, Muslims should ensure that they are clean. Therefore, before praying, I perform a special washing routine called 'wudu'. Wudu involves washing the hands, face, feet, arms, mouth, ears and head, but it is more than just washing; it is about preparing my mind and spirit so that I am ready to talk with God.

**Sabeel**

## **THINK ABOUT IT!**

3.  Use the information you have read in this lesson, and your own knowledge and ideas, to produce a spider diagram about water. You will need to mention religious understandings of water, non-religious understanding and information, and your own personal understanding. You may find it helpful to colour code your spider diagram.

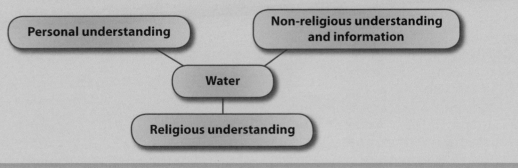

In this lesson you will:
- examine the different ways in which stories are used
- evaluate the reliability of stories
- investigate the idea that stories can be used to express 'truth'.

## KEY WORDS

**Cultures** the different beliefs and practices of societies

**Epic** a long story or poem which tells of a famous person or event

**Aboriginal** the first, native people of Australia

**Deities** god and goddesses in Hinduism

**Scholars** great thinkers who have developed our understanding

**Narrative** a spoken or written way of expressing ideas

In modern Western societies, many people think of 'stories' or 'myths' as the opposite of 'truth'. People often think that something is only 'true' if it really happened and therefore 'stories' are 'made up'. Sometimes people use the word 'story' to mean something that is not important or even a 'lie'. In this lesson you are going to look more carefully at these ideas and explore different understandings of 'story'.

## WHY DO PEOPLE TELL STORIES?

In many **cultures**, stories are often told to express complicated beliefs about the world and about how people should behave.

If we want to make sense of the world around us, and our fellow human beings, we may need to realize that stories can be very powerful ways of conveying what people believe to be true.

In my Hindu culture, we have many stories about hundreds of heroes and **deities**. I have heard them since I was a child and I love them! We do not think that the 'truth' of these stories means whether they 'really happened'. They can tell us important things about the world and ourselves – that is what makes them 'true' or not.

**Maya**

## THE EPIC OF GILGAMESH

This is one of the oldest written stories in the world. It was written on clay tablets about 2000 BCE. It tells of the adventures of a king called Gilgamesh, who lived in Sumeria (an ancient country that was part of what we now call Iraq) about 2750 BCE. The **epic** includes a story of a flood, which covered the whole world, and tells of one person and his family who survived. This is an example of a story told to try and explain the mysteries of the world. Ancient people tried to explain why disasters such as floods took place. In trying to understand why things happened, they told stories about gods who controlled the world. This story of the flood has been told again and again by many cultures because people wanted to answer these important questions using their own versions of the story.

## ● DREAMTIME

Some stories have been spoken rather than written. The **Aboriginal** people of Australia tell stories about the Dreamtime, the time in which they believe the world was created. In these stories, animals and the land are shown to be of great importance. These stories are ways of expressing the respect that Aborigine people show for the natural world around them. The stories have been handed down by word of mouth, generation by generation, for thousands of years.

> As an atheist, I believe that people have told religious stories over a long time to explain things that puzzled or scared them. That is why they imagined a god or gods. For me, only scientific theories are really reliable. I am also a Humanist, though, so I think it is important to know about these stories and understand how different people make sense of the world.

**Kerrie**

## ● WHY SHOULD WE BOTHER ABOUT STORIES?

Even in modern Western societies, some **scholars** are saying that we should take stories more seriously. Another word for story is **narrative**. Some scholars claim that finding out 'what really happened' means that you have to listen to different people's narratives. They are saying that people can understand events in different ways, even if they are actually there. People tell their version of what happened and this is their 'narrative'. This suggests that the difference between 'stories' and 'what really happened' might be more complicated than most people think!

Here is an example.

Mike and Naomi are describing the same meeting and yet they tell very different stories.

*Mike:*

'I met with Naomi at the park on Monday. It is a cool place, but it was horrible, miserable weather. She was in a really bad mood, so I was very careful about what I said and tried to cheer her up. She said that I still had her CD, but I know I gave it back to her the other day, just after we had

been to see that excellent film. The trouble with me is that I am too soft; all our friends say so. I will probably end up buying her another CD even though I know I gave it back to her. They are a rubbish band anyway.'

*Naomi:*

'I saw Mike yesterday in that stupid park. I asked him for my CD back. I really wanted to hear it again, that band is so good. He said he had not got it – typical! He said he gave it back after that boring film we saw, but I know he did not. I bet he has lost it. Still, there was no need for him to get so touchy about it. I should have known he would, all our friends say he can be a bit aggressive. It is a shame, because I was in a really good mood until then because it was such a lovely autumn day.'

We have looked carefully at what we mean by 'stories' because they are used by religions to express religious beliefs. In the next lesson we will examine some of these. The ideas explored in this lesson help us to realize that there might be more to 'stories' than we first thought.

### THINK ABOUT IT!

1. Read Mike and Naomi's stories.
   a) What are the differences in their descriptions of what happened? What do you think are the reasons for these differences?
   b) Decide which parts of their account are fact and which are opinion. Compare your results with a partner. How does this show us the difficulties in saying 'what really happened'?

In this lesson you will:
● examine the ways in which religions express their beliefs through stories
● explain how the **Gospel** birth stories show important Christian beliefs about Jesus.

## ● 'THAT'S THE STORY OF MY LIFE!'

People often use this phrase to describe something that they think is always happening to them. As we found out in the last lesson, 'story' can mean many things. It does not just mean 'something that did not really happen'. For instance, when we refer to our 'life story', we are talking about events that have happened to us. To describe the 'story of your life' is to decide what are the most significant events and what they mean to you. Stories can be a way of saying what is important to you.

A **myth** is a story that explains the relationship between humanity and a higher power, for example, god. Myths are often told to explain events in history or the natural world. They sometimes have a religious meaning. What these stories all have in common, however, is that they convey beliefs about God and/or the world.

The word 'myth' is often used to describe an idea that is not really true, so I am not happy about the stories in my holy book, the **Qur'an**, being described as 'myths'. I do believe, though, that we can learn important things from these stories. There are also stories about the life of the Prophet Muhammad. These teach us how to behave as good Muslims. Such a story is called a **Hadith**.

**Sabeel**

### THINK ABOUT IT!

1. This is a modern Christian picture of the birth of Jesus.
   a) What do you notice about it?
   b) What can we learn about the meaning of the birth story for Christians by the way that this picture is drawn?

# BIRTH NARRATIVES

Many religious traditions tell stories about the births of important people. These stories often describe remarkable things happening around this person's birth in order to show how special this person is. Such accounts can be called 'birth narratives', 'nativity stories' or 'myths'.

You might be familiar with the Christian story of Jesus' birth because it is told at Christmas. Although it is a very well known story, not everyone realizes that there are actually two different written versions of Jesus' birth in the Christian Gospels. If we study these carefully, we can see that they are expressing important beliefs that Christians have about Jesus.

> As a Christian, I enjoy the Christmas story about Mary and Joseph in Bethlehem, but, for me, the important part of the story is that Jesus was born in a stable. I think this shows that God came into the world as a poor, homeless person rather than a powerful king.
>
> **Kim**

## THINK ABOUT IT!

**2.** Read the two versions of Jesus' birth in the Christian Bible.

*Matthew 1:18 – Matthew 2:23*
Mary was to be married to Joseph. But before they were married she became pregnant by the Holy Spirit. An angel appeared to Joseph in a dream and said to him, 'Joseph, do not be afraid to take Mary as your wife. She will give birth to a son and you are to name him Jesus.' This happened to fulfill what God had said through the prophet.

After Jesus was born in Bethlehem, Magi came from the east to Jerusalem and asked, 'Where is the one who has been born king of the Jews? We saw his star and have come to worship him.' Mary and Joseph then had to escape with Jesus to Egypt so that King Herod would not kill him. When it was safe to return, Joseph was told by an angel in a dream to go and live in Nazareth.

*Luke 1:26 – 31, Luke 2: 1–20, Luke 2:39*
God sent the angel Gabriel to Nazareth, to Mary, who was going to be married to Joseph. The angel went to her and said, 'Greetings, you who are most blessed! The Lord is with you. You will give birth to a son, and you are to call him Jesus.'

Caesar Augustus decided that a census should be taken of the entire Roman world. And so everyone went to his own town to register.

So Joseph and Mary went from Nazareth to Bethlehem. While they were there, the time came for the baby to be born, and Mary gave birth to a son. She wrapped him in cloths and placed him in a manger, because there was no room in the inn. Angels told nearby shepherds of Jesus' birth and they came to see the baby. After all this, Mary, Joseph and Jesus returned to Nazareth.

**a)** What are the main differences in the two stories?
**b)** Why do you think there are differences between the stories?
**c)** Although there are differences, what are the main ideas that *both* stories contain?
**d)** How do these parts of the story show what Christians believe about Jesus?

### KEY WORDS

**Gospel** the first four books of the New Testament: Matthew, Mark, Luke and John

**Myth** a story told to express beliefs about God or the world

**Qur'an** the holy book of Islam

**Hadiths** sayings and traditions of Muhammad

In this lesson you will:
- interpret some visual symbols
- discuss how many meanings can be expressed in one visual symbol
- express your own ideas using visual symbols.

So far, we have looked at the idea that symbols can be understood like a code. They can seem very confusing if we do not know the key to that code. This idea can help us to interpret some of the visual symbols that religions use.

A visual symbol may have many meanings that are 'decoded' when we understand more about a religion and how the followers of that religion see the world.

## ● THE CRESCENT MOON AND STAR

Here are just two of the many understandings that Muslims have associated with the crescent moon and star.

1 The moon and stars have been used to help guide travellers through the dark for thousands of years. Some Muslims see the teachings of Islam as a guide to their journey through life, helping them to see the safe path.

2 The moon plays a key role in the Islamic calendar. The first sighting of the new or crescent moon marks the beginning of each month. The new moon also marks the beginning and ending of Ramadan, the period of fasting.

This symbol has commonly been understood as representing Islam. Both the crescent moon and the five-pointed star have many different meanings for Muslims.

### THINK ABOUT IT!

1. **a)** Draw a crescent moon and star in the centre of a spider diagram. Write down as many different meanings as possible that you associate with the moon and stars.
   **b)** Compare your ideas with a classmate; share and record any different ideas.

## ● AUM

Not all visual symbols are in the form of a picture. In Hinduism, one important visual symbol is also a piece of writing.

The symbol opposite is written in the ancient language of Sanskrit. It is often referred to as 'Aum' because it is made up of three letters of the Sanskrit alphabet, and the closest translation of them is a, u and m. Many Hindus believe that 'Aum' was the first sound of the universe and so this sound can help them to feel more connected to God and the universe.

Some Hindus see these letters as representing the **Trimurti** – three of the many Hindu deities that Hindus believe have a very important role in keeping the universe in order. They are: Brahma, the creator; Vishnu, the preserver; and Shiva, the destroyer. These three deities are responsible for the universe and so some Hindus would also see 'Aum' as a symbol of the universe as a whole.

'Aum' is not only used as a visual symbol but also as a spoken one. It is often spoken at the beginning of worship. Many Hindus believe that when 'Aum' is pronounced correctly, it can stimulate the body, mind and soul , helping them to prepare to talk with God. These ideas are remembered and re-enforced when people look at the visual symbol.

**Aum is the main symbol of Hinduism. It represents God and the sound of creation.**

### KEY WORDS

**Trimurti**  the three gods of creation, sustaining and destruction - Brahma, Vishnu and Shiva

**Brahman**  the supreme God in Hinduism, understood to be ultimate reality

### THINK ABOUT IT!

2.  Visual symbols are used by religions to express a variety of messages.
    a)  Decide on a positive message of your own, for example, 'I hope for world peace,' or, 'I think friends and family are very important.'
    b)  Turn this message into a visual symbol by replacing the key words in your message with images that you think represent the meanings of those words. Give a brief explanation of your choice of images.
    c)  Now link the images. You might find that two or more of your images could be joined together, or even replaced by another image.
    d)  When you are finished, show your visual symbol to a friend. How easily can they see your original meaning?

In this lesson you will:
● examine the ways in which religious art is symbolic
● demonstrate how Hindu images express important Hindu beliefs.

This is a painting of the Hindu deity, Ganesha. People who do not know about Hinduism might find it difficult to understand what this image means. Many Hindus respect Ganesha as the 'remover of obstacles'. Ganesha has an elephant's head and four arms.

## ? THINK ABOUT IT!

1. Look at the the objects that surround Ganesha. How does this show us what the artist feels about him?

## ● EVERY PICTURE TELLS A STORY

This is particularly true of religious pictures. Religions have produced beautiful art for thousands of years. These images are not just for decoration. Sometimes religions need to express ideas and beliefs that are very difficult to put into words.

Visual images can sometimes show these ideas more easily than language can. The pictures are symbolic. If we learn how to decode or interpret them, we can have a better understanding of what they are saying and what they mean to the people who produce and use them. As an example of this, we are going to examine pictures from Hinduism.

Religions show their beliefs about God in different ways. Some religions believe that it is wrong to try and draw any pictures of God. Islam, for example, teaches that **Allah** is too great to be imagined. Muslims believe that it is a sin to try and draw any images of Allah.

Instead, Islam has produced beautiful examples of geometric patterns and **calligraphy**, which uses the words of their holy book, the Qur'an.

## KEY WORDS

**Allah** the Arabic name for God in Islam

**Calligraphy** the fine art of handwriting

**Ahimsa** non-violence, respect for life

## HINDU ART

Many Hindus believe in one supreme God whom they call **Brahman**. They worship Brahman in various forms. Brahman is one but can be expressed in many different ways and is represented by hundreds of deities. Pictures of these deities express belief in the greatness of Brahman by showing that he can be seen in everything.

Here are two key Hindu beliefs.

1  A central Hindu concept is **ahimsa** or non-violence, and Hinduism teaches respect for all forms of life. Most Hindus are vegetarians.

2  The Hindu greeting is 'namaste'. This means, 'I greet you., the eternal soul within the heart' Hinduism teaches that God, who is also Brahman is everywhere, including the heart helping Hindus to have a very personal realtionship with God.

Look at this piece of Islamic art. Calligraphy like this appears in many mosques.

This is an example of one of the many expressions of Brahman. She is the deity Durga.

### THINK ABOUT IT!

2.  Look carefully at the picture of Durga.
    a)  How does it show what Hindus believe about God and the world?
    b)  Which parts of the picture symbolize Hindu beliefs?
    c)  How would Hindu beliefs about seeing the sacred in all forms of life affect the way they treat other people and the environment? Write a short paragraph to summarize your ideas.

# 2.6 SYMBOLIC ACTIONS

In this lesson you will:
- analyse the ways that symbolic actions are regularly used
- explore the meanings these actions convey
- discuss and reflect upon the effect of symbolic actions throughout a person's life.

**KEY WORDS**

**Shahadah** declaration of faith in Allah

Symbolic actions are a regular part of our lives. Did you know that one of the most commonly used symbolic actions, the handshake, is thought to date back more than 600 years?

Every day, around the world, people shake hands. However, handshakes have not always been so widely used and understood.

In Europe, the handshake was originally a symbol used by medieval knights. By extending an open hand, the knights could show that they were not hiding a weapon and did not pose a threat.

Today, this simple action is used in many different ways:
- as a friendly gesture to greet someone or say goodbye
- to identify a person as a member of a particular group
- to seal an agreement.

**THINK ABOUT IT!**

1. The handshake is a widely used and understood symbol – how would we get by without it? Think of one other gesture that we could use as a positive greeting. It must be appropriate to use in the way that we would use a handshake and you must think about how another person would react to your symbolic action.

## ● CELEBRATING USING SYMBOLS

Symbols are often used at certain key points in life. For example, both religious and non-religious groups see birth as a special event and a celebration. Although the celebrations vary, they often use symbolic actions, gestures and words. These actions communicate the idea that life is special and express hope that the child will be fortunate, healthy, and will grow up to be a responsible adult.

Below are two accounts of symbolic actions that begin soon after birth and continue throughout life.

As Muslims, when my brother was born, my family and friends got together to welcome him into the world. Before we saw him, my father had whispered the **Shahadah** into his ear in Arabic: 'There is no God but Allah, Muhammad is the messenger of Allah.' My father read the adhan (call to prayer) into the ear of my brother which is an important part of the birth ceremony. These words will accompany my brother through his life, he will hear them daily as part of the adhan, or call to prayer, and they will be the last words spoken to him before he dies.

After whispering the Shahadah, my father wrote 'Allah' on my brother's tongue in honey. This is because we hope that when my brother can speak, his words will be sweet and please Allah.

**Sabeel**

I do not remember my own baptism because I was only a few months old at the time. The decision to bring me into the Roman Catholic community was made for me by my parents. My godparents were there too, and made promises to support my parents and me.

When I enter my church, I make the sign of the cross using water that is held in small stone bowls called stoops near the main entrance. This is a special action for me. The water reminds me of my baptism and the sign of the cross is a symbol of my belief that Jesus died for our sins and rose again. Again, this reminds me of my baptism, when I 'died' to a life of sin and was reborn into a life with God.

**Kim**

### THINK ABOUT IT!

2. Read through each of the accounts above.
   a) For each of the accounts, give one example of a symbolic action and what that action means.
   b) How is each action re-enforced throughout a person's life?
   c) In these accounts, the symbolic actions are part of decisions made on behalf of the child soon after birth. Give three examples of actions that have been taken on your behalf. How do you think these actions have affected your life so far? How might they affect it in the future?

In this lesson you will:
- investigate the use of a range of symbols used in worship
- analyse how different symbols can be combined to express a key religious belief.

In this chapter you have analysed how different religious beliefs and ideas are communicated through a variety of symbols, including stories, images, objects and actions. Sometimes a number of these different symbols are used together. Although they each have a significance of their own, they play a small part in expressing a larger message.

## WHAT IS A RITUAL?

Religious **rituals** are an important example of this idea. A ritual is an action, or series of actions, that follow a certain pattern. This pattern is repeated regularly and can form the basis of religious worship.

To begin understanding the whole ritual, we may need to investigate the meanings behind individual symbols being used.

In Hinduism, the most common form of worship, called **puja**, uses a variety of images, objects and symbolic actions. Most Hindus perform puja at least once a day; this might be at a shrine in their own home or at a temple. Puja is one way in which Hindus show love and affection to the deities.

This photo shows how a puja shrine might be laid out in a Hindu home.

## ● PERFORMING PUJA

Puja involves making offerings to one or more of the many deities. However, individual Hindus perform puja in slightly different ways. For example, the deities that the offerings are made to and what the offerings are could well be very different from one household or temple to another.

1 An image, or **murti**, of the deity Durga, who is being worshipped

2 A bowl of water

3 Some flowers

4 Some fruit

5 Incense

6 A bell

7 The symbol 'Aum'

8 Candles

> ### KEY WORDS
>
> **Ritual** an action, or series of actions, that follow a certain pattern
>
> **Puja** Hindu act of worship to show devotion to God
>
> **Murti** figures which represent gods and goddesses in Hinduism

### THINK ABOUT IT!

1. Use the list above to identify which symbols within the picture of the puja shrine can be linked with each of the headings below. Some symbols may fit under more than one heading.
   a) Three gifts to the deity showing how we are provided for by nature.
   b) Four symbols representing the elements earth, water, air and fire.
   c) Five symbols representing the senses hearing, touch, taste, sight and smell.
   d) The focus of worship.
   e) A symbol to help focus the body and mind.
   f) A symbol representing the sacred universe.

In Hinduism, there is very little division between life and religion; almost every aspect of life is affected by religious beliefs. As a daily form of worship, puja helps to express this idea, using a variety of symbols to help illustrate how God can be experienced throughout life.

### THINK ABOUT IT!

2. How do you express the ideas and beliefs that are important to you?
   List three ideas or beliefs that you think are important and explain how this is shown in your words or actions. Do you always show these ideas clearly?

### What this task is all about:

1 Use the guidelines below to draw a mandala called 'A world of beliefs'. Use symbols to make the mandala. You can use religious symbols like the ones shown in the chapter or create your own.

2 Write an explanation of your mandala, describing why you have chosen your symbols, what they mean and how they can be interpreted.

### What you need to do to complete the task:

1 Use the template on worksheet 2.21. All the spaces in the mandala need to be filled with symbols that are relevant to 'a world of beliefs'.

2 Your written work should explain the meanings of the symbols and why they are being used. Refer to the religious beliefs expressed by the symbols. Give examples from your own ideas and experience. Discuss how the symbols can be interpreted. Give careful reasons for your ideas and opinions, using examples from different religions and worldviews. Show that you understand the ideas in this chapter.

### Hints and tips

- Remember that symbols can mean different things.
- Do not be afraid to give your own opinion, but always give reasons for your ideas.
- Show respect for the importance of religious symbols for the believers.
- You can find examples by going to www.heinemann. co.uk/hotlinks express code 7177P.
- Make your mandala as original as possible.

| TO ACHIEVE | YOU WILL NEED TO |
| --- | --- |
| Level 3 | Use a variety of symbols. Describe the symbols you use and explain why you have chosen them. |
| Level 4 | Use a variety of well-chosen symbols. Describe their meaning by using personal ideas and by referring to different religions and worldviews. |
| Level 5 | Use a variety of well-chosen symbols, showing some originality in your ideas. Explain the meaning of the symbols by not only using personal experiences but also referring to the wider community and world issues. |
| Level 6 | Use a variety of well-chosen symbols, showing originality in your ideas and giving examples from several different religions and worldviews. Show how the symbols can be interpreted in different ways, using several ideas from this chapter. |

# 3 WHAT DO PEOPLE BELIEVE ABOUT GOD?

## THE BIGGER PICTURE

Whether you believe in God or not, it is important to understand that for millions of people 'God' means the most powerful and important force in the world. We will be exploring reasons for believing and not believing in God, and what difference this might make to people's lives and behaviour. Exploring these different ideas can help you reflect on your own beliefs and how these might affect what you do.

## WHAT?

You will:
- identify what religious beliefs and worldviews there are about God
- explain the importance of understanding people's beliefs about God
- make links between people's beliefs about God and how they live
- describe the different ways that people express their beliefs about the nature and existence of God.

## HOW?

By:
- looking carefully at religious and non-religious ideas about God
- comparing evidence and arguments about the nature and existence of God
- describing how beliefs about God affects people's lives.

## WHY?

Because:
- in order to understand other people, you need to know about the beliefs that matter to them
- to do this, you need to be able to analyse how beliefs about God affect key decisions in many people's lives
- this could help you understand some of the major events in the world around you and perhaps lead you to consider which beliefs are important to you.

## KEY IDEAS

- For centuries, people have debated whether there is a God and, if so, what God is like.
- 'God' can mean different things to different people. Understanding what people believe about God or the **sacred** can help you understand why they think and act the way they do.
- Most people in the world believe that there is a divine being who created and maintains the world. Most refer to this being as 'God'
- In modern times, many people are questioning whether God exists.

These people all believe in God, but God means different things to each of them.

## KEY WORDS

| | | | |
|---|---|---|---|
| Sacred | Disciplined | Kosher | Atheist |
| Agnostic | Allah | Shahadah | Monotheistic |
| Trinity | Qur'an | Guru | Shema |
| Creator | Guru Granth Sahib | Ik Onkar | Omnipotent |
| Unity | Mool Mantar | Kirpan | Omnipresent |
| Omniscient | Gurdwara | Langar | Torah |
| Mitzvot | Brahman | Theist | Tawhid |

In this lesson you will:
- use specific terminology relating to beliefs about God
- show an understanding of arguments for and against belief in God.

**H**ave you ever wondered whether God really exists or not? If God does exist, could it ever be proved? In fact, does it even need to be proved?

Think for a moment about what you imagine God would look like if God existed. What do you see? We often think of God in human terms – perhaps even as an elderly man with a big beard, sitting on a cloud. It is easier for us to imagine God this way than trying to imagine an invisible 'force'. Other people do not believe in God at all.

Imagine that God is a 'super being', an invisible force. What would you want God to be able to do? What do you think God would know? Would God be powerful? Would God be a good listener? Maybe God would be female. Why are all of these things important?

## ● DOES EVERYONE BELIEVE IN GOD?

Some people believe in God, some do not believe in God at all and others are unsure whether or not they think God exists. There are names for these different groups of people:

A **theist** is someone who believes in the existence of God or gods.

An **agnostic** is someone who is unsure whether God exists or not because there is not enough evidence for us to know this.

An **atheist** is someone who believes that there is no God and no possibility of God existing.

**God creating the universe, a painting by William Blake**

### THINK ABOUT IT!

1. Using the definitions above to help you, write one reason why a person might be an atheist, a theist or an agnostic. Think about things that happen in the world – is there anything that you have read about in the news recently or watched on television that might affect whether or not a person believes in God?

## WHAT ARGUMENTS ARE THERE FOR AND AGAINST THE EXISTENCE OF GOD?

We know that different people have different beliefs about the existence of God. They may base these beliefs on things that happen around them or on experiences that they themselves have had. Some people argue that belief in God comes from a need to have something powerful we can turn to. Some would say that it is important to cope with life's difficulties without imagining a God who can help us out.

## WHAT MIGHT A HUMANIST SAY?

Humanists believe that there is no God. They would also say that kindness and goodness can come from human behaviour and they do not have to rely on a God to tell them what to do. They might say that it is better to help others because you think it is is right rather than to do it because God says so or because you want to go to heaven.

Whatever our own beliefs, it is important to understand and listen to those of other people, and to consider how they have formed their opinion.

> **KEY WORDS**
>
> **Theist** someone who believes in the existence of a God or Gods
>
> **Agnostic** someone who is unsure whether God exists or not
>
> **Atheist** someone who does not believe in the existence of a God

### THINK ABOUT IT!

2. Look at the image of the tsunami that occurred after Christmas in 2004. Images such as this can make it hard to believe that God exists. Using the ideas about God that you have looked at earlier in the lesson, write a paragraph explaining why this picture could make people doubt the existence of God. Do you think a theist, atheist and agnostic would agree with you? Why?

3. How could you argue that God does exist even though bad things happen in the world? Below are some examples of how people do this. With a partner, try to rank them in order of most convincing to least convincing. Give a reason for each of your choices. Do any of these arguments stand up to interrogation?
   - God gave people free will. They can act however they want!
   - God is testing our faith to see if we believe in God even after bad things happen.
   - God would rather that we chose to do good things instead of being forced to.
   - God is like a parent who wants the best for you but cannot stop bad things happening.
   - The actions of God are beyond our understanding.
   - God knows that suffering leads to good deeds such as heroism and generosity.

# 3.2 WHAT DO IMAGES OF GOD SYMBOLIZE?

In this lesson you will:
- explore how **sacred** images help people to understand God
- suggest meanings for symbols associated with God
- express your own ideas about how God is symbolized.

Whether people believe in 'the sacred' or not, most of us have some sort of image or idea of what God is believed to be like. However, that idea will be very dependant on our culture (where we grew up, the main religions in our part of the world, our parents' beliefs and so on). For example, children in India or Japan might have very different ideas about the image of God compared to some children in England because they have grown up in different places, have parents with different beliefs, or have read different books and watched different films and TV. When we look at images of God, it is important to think about the 'culture' of the people who have made the images because this will help us to break the codes.

Many people see God as an old man with a long white beard, sitting on clouds. We see these sorts of images almost every day, from things like paintings in churches, pictures in books to films and cartoons. This view of God is very common in Christianity but is actually far more ancient, being based on Zeus of Ancient Greek god of the sky and ruler of all other gods. The reason why this Greek image of God has had such an influence on images of the Christian God is probably becuase the Greek ideas, and the Roman ideas that followed them, have been very influential throughout history, from the time of the first Christians right up to today.

A modern interpretation of God - what symbolizm has the film maker used?

## THINK ABOUT IT!

1. People often create images of God to show their ideas about God's power and nature. Look at the images on this page and write down your thoughts and ideas about what the artist is saying about God. You may use the words in the box below to help you.

| | |
|---|---|
| Loving | Intimidating |
| Scary | Friendly |
| Wise | Human-like |
| Serious | Loving |
| Gentle | Unnatural |
| Powerful | Peaceful |

2. a) What symbols are used in each of the images?
   b) What do you think these symbols represent?

## ● WHY IS GOD OFTEN SHOWN AS A MAN?

Have you ever noticed that people often talk of God as being male? In Christianity, God is often called 'Father', 'Lord', 'Master' and 'King'. Is there a danger that this might give a very one-sided idea of what God is like? Referring to God as male, can be seen to make men more like God than women, something that many people feel today is unfair and sexist. To challenge this, some Christians also refer to God as 'Mother' to emphasize God's loving, caring and life-giving nature. In some religions such as Hinduism and paganism, the sacred is often deliberately imagined as being female (as with the deity Durga in Hinduism and with the concept of the Earth Mother in paganism).

### THINK ABOUT IT!

3. Look at the images of the sacred on these pages. Why do you think the artists have chosen to represent God in these ways? What do you think the artists are trying to say about the sacred?

4. Many people think of God as being male and use language such as 'Father' to describe God. Why do you think this is? Explain your answer.

5. Write a response to the following question and link it to your learning about the nature of God: 'If God is female, she can do the job just as well as a man.' Do you agree or disagree? Give reasons for your answer.

### KEY WORDS

**Sacred** another word for God or the divine

🎧 Why do you think this sixteenth-century artist has portrayed God in this way?

🎧 What do you think this painting says about the artists' view of God?

In this lesson you will:
● investigate the Christian concept of the **Trinity**
● make links between belief in God and how Christians might treat others and the world around them.

Think about yourself: even though you are one person, you might have different roles in life. For example, a girl could be a daughter, a sister and a student – but she is still the same person. What roles do you have in your life?

Think of something else that can also come in three forms. If you need a clue, think about water.

Christians are **monotheistic**. This means that they believe there is only one God. In the same way that you can take on different roles in your life, Christians believe that there can be different aspects to God's nature. However, they believe that God is still one being and not three different gods. This is known as the Trinity – God can be Father, Son and Holy Spirit.

## KEY WORDS

**Trinity** the Christian belief that there are three persons within one God: the Father, the Son and the Holy Spirit

**Monotheistic** belief in only one God

**Creator** the person who brings something into existence

## THINK ABOUT IT!

1. Using the knowledge you already have about Christianity, what do you think the roles Father, Son and Holy Spirit might mean for Christians?

2. Look at the following explanations of each aspect of the Trinity:
   - 'Christians believe that Jesus was God in human form.'
   - 'A force that Christians believe can be everywhere and may even perform miracles in the world and act within the world.'
   - 'Christians might think of God as a parental being or force, perhaps in heaven.'

   Which aspect of the Trinity do you think fits with each explanation? Try and match them up. Now copy and fill out the following table.

| Aspect of the Trinity | Explanation | ? |
|---|---|---|
| Father | | |
| Son | | |
| Holy Spirit | | |

3. Having investigated the nature of God before, how might the aspects of the Trinity relate to other Christian beliefs about God?

4. Here are some words that could be used to describe God:

| | |
|---|---|
| **Creator** | All-powerful |
| Loving | Good |
| All-present (present everywhere) | All-knowing |

How do these relate to the ideas of Father, Son and Holy Spirit? Place each of the words in the third column of the table after deciding where you think they should go. For example, if God can be everywhere at once as the Holy Spirit, this could mean God is all-present What else could it mean? Some of the words can go in more than one column.

5. If Christians believe that God is kind and loving, knows everything, created the world and can do anything, how might this affect the way they live their lives? Consider the following and write a couple of sentences about each:
   a) the way Christians treat the environment
   b) the way that Christians treat one another
   c) the way Christians act in times of suffering.

🎧 **This person is collecting for St Johns Ambulance. Why do Christians try to give money to charity?**

In this lesson you will:
- ask questions about Jewish beliefs about the nature of God
- use religious vocabulary to describe Jewish beliefs about God
- express your own opinions on the importance of following rules in Judaism.

## ● WHAT DO JEWS BELIEVE ABOUT GOD?

'Hear O Israel: the Lord is our God, the Lord is one.'

This is the first part of the **Shema**, a Jewish prayer that is said every morning and evening. Belief in one God is one of the most important ideas in Judaism because it holds everything in the universe together. Jews believe that God created and understands everything in the universe – the planets, the animals, the plants and the people.

The Jewish belief in one God reflects an understanding that there is **unity** in the world. Jews believe God is all-powerful (omnipotent), all-knowing (omniscient) and all-present (omnipresent). They also believe God is benevolent (good and loving) and cares deeply for humans.

In Judaism, it is very difficult to describe God because Jews believe that any words limit the understanding of something that is believed to be completely *outside* human understanding. Jews believe God is far too powerful and beyond human understanding to be drawn, so there are no images of God in Judaism.

So if God is infinite and outside human understanding how can Jews become closer to God?

**THINK ABOUT IT!**

1. Why do you think Jews say the Shema every morning and evening?

2. Why might Jews want to communicate with God at different points in the day?

All **synagogues** store a copy of the Torah scrolls. The scrolls are often covered by a decorated piece of cloth with a shield and set of bells to act as a crown.

## ● GROWING CLOSER TO GOD

Jews believe that to become closer to God, they must lead their lives the way God expects them to. They know what is expected of them because God has given them teachings and laws to follow.

More than 3000 years ago, God chose a man called Moses and gave him 613 rules (called **mitzvot**), starting with the Ten Commandments. Moses is seen as the most important Jewish prophet because he spent his life teaching and leading the Jewish people. He also wrote down everything God taught him and these writings form the most important part of the Jewish holy book, called the **Torah** (meaning 'instruction').

## ● HOW CAN FOLLOWING RULES HELP JEWS TO 'KNOW' GOD?

Following God's teachings in the Torah and mitzvot lie at the heart of practicing Judaism. In fact, Jews believe that when they follow the mitzvot, they are communicating with God. The mitzvot teach Jews about every aspect of life: justice, praying, festivals, weddings, and food.

Following the mitzvot helps Jews lead a **disciplined** life. Some mitzvot are seen as tests of faith, so following them also makes people's faith in God stronger (for example, only eating certain types of food, called **kosher**).

Following the mitzvot is also one way of showing deep respect for God in every part of a Jew's life. For example, many Jews will never write the word 'God'. Instead they will spell it 'G-d'. This is because one mitzvah, contained in the Ten Commandments, states, 'Do not take G-d's name in vain.' For Jews, this means never writing the name down in full and never pronouncing the name except in worship.

The Torah commands that Jews should rest one day each week, because God created the world in six days and rested on the seventh. Jews call this day of rest **Shabbat**. Because it is a day of rest there are many laws in the Torah about types of activities which should not be done. One of these laws says that no work should be completed on Shabbat. Many Jews take this to mean that nothing electrical (for example television, light switches) shoul be switched on because that would involve completing an electrical circuit. Many Jews do not use any electricity on Shabbat, creating a very peceful environment at home.

A Jewish man wearing Tefillin. Tefillin are small leather boxes which contain the Shema prayer and are attached to the head and arms as a sign of devotion to God.

### KEY WORDS

**Shema** a prayer used by Jews maintaining belief in one God

**Unity** the state of being harmonious and united

**Mitzot (singular mitzvah)** Jewish religious laws, good deeds or duties

**Torah** Jewish Books of the Law, the first five books of the Tenakh

**Disciplined** controlled behaviour that follows rules

**Kosher** food seen as pure and acceptable by Jews according to the Torah

**Shabbat** Jewish name for the holy day also known as the Sabbath

### THINK ABOUT IT!

3. Putting 'God' in the centre, create a spider diagram to explain Jewish beliefs about God. You should include beliefs about the nature of God and ideas about how Jews become closer to God.

4. 'The Torah is thousands of years old, so is out of date. The mitzvot should not be that important today.' Do you agree? Write arguments from more than one point of view.

# 3.5 THE ISLAMIC VIEW OF GOD

In this lesson you will:
- reflect on how Islamic ideas about **Allah** are expressed through artwork
- interpret different Islamic views of Allah.

For many Muslims, life can be seen as an incredible task such as crossing a desert. it might be very difficult, with many risks, but it is possible for those who follow Allah's message because they will be given everything they need to survive and led to safety.

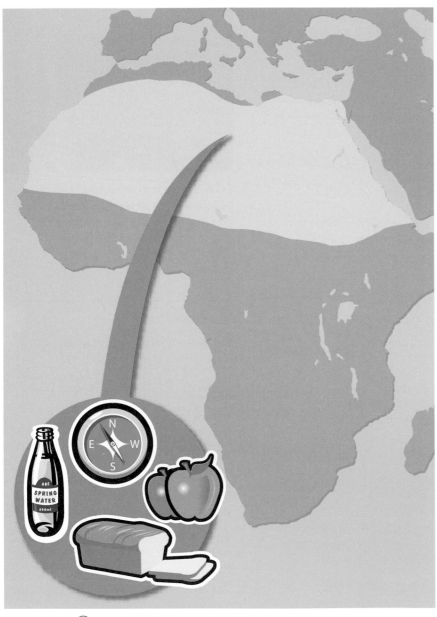

🎧 **What would you want to take with you on a long, difficult journey, for example, if you were travelling across the Sahara Desert?**

## ● THE SHAHADAH – A STATEMENT OF BELIEF

**'**I witness that there is no God but Allah and that Muhammad is the Messenger of Allah.**'**

In Chapter 1, you were introduced to the **Shahadah** (see page 14). This is a statement that contains one of the most important beliefs in Islam. 'Shahadah' is an Arabic word that can mean 'witness'. Many Muslims repeat the Shahadah every day.

There are two key statements made in the Shahadah:

1   Allah is the one true God. There are no other deities. All life comes from Allah and all life is connected with Allah – this belief is known as **tawhid**, which means 'unity'.
2   Allah has spoken to humankind through his messenger, Muhammad. Allah's message is recorded in the **Qur'an**, the Muslim holy book, which is sometimes called Kalam Allah (the Speech of God).

### KEY WORDS

**Allah**  the Arabic name for God in Islam

**Shahadah**  Islamic declaration of faith in Allah

**Tawhid**  belief in the oneness of Allah

**Qur'an**  the holy book of Islam

## ● TAWHID – EVERYWHERE, EVERY DAY

Islam teaches that Allah is responsible for all creation; therefore there is a connection between all creation and Allah. Some Muslims believe that this connection with Allah means that humankind and the natural world reflect the nature of Allah, their creator.

Many Muslims would also say that because Allah is the source of all creation and without Allah there would be nothing, it is impossible for some things to happen with Allah and some things to happen without Allah – Allah is what unites everything.

Below is an example of how the idea of tawhid has been expressed using Islamic art.

**THINK ABOUT IT!**

1.  Look at the example of Islamic art on this page carefully.
    a) What shapes can you see in the artwork?
    b) Which shapes do you think might be the most important and why?
    c) What do you notice about the way that the shapes are formed?
    d) How might this image help to explain the idea of tawhid?

## ● TAWHID – TALKING TO GOD

In the Qur'an, it states that there are 99 names by which humans can know Allah – each one reveals something different about the nature of Allah. Some Muslims believe that there are still more names for Allah but that they are beyond human knowledge.

Many Muslims believe that it is possible to talk to Allah. Some people would say that this is similar to a conversation, with speaking and listening on both sides.

Other people would say that although humans can talk to Allah, Allah is beyond our understanding, making a conversation very difficult. However, it is important to Muslims that Allah is recognized as having many qualities, all of which are connected but different. When talking to or about Allah, Muslims are careful to refer to Allah using the most appropriate name.

**THINK ABOUT IT!**

2.  Below are six of the 99 names for Allah. For each name, describe the circumstances that you think would make that the most appropriate name to use in addressing Allah.

    The Most Compassionate     All Peaceful, the one who makes peace
    The King     The Almighty
    The Most Holy     The Forgiver

3.  How might the 99 names for Allah make it easier for Muslims to talk to Allah every day?

In this lesson you will:
● examine Sikh beliefs about God
● explain how Sikhs live out their beliefs in everyday life
● raise and answer questions about God during a class debate.

Many people think that equality and justice are important ideas. For Sikhs, they are central to their beliefs about God and humanity.

## ● 'WE ARE ALL ONE, CREATED BY THE ONE CREATOR OF ALL CREATION'

Belief in one creator God is central to Sikhism. Sikhs believe that because God created everyone, everyone is equal. For example, Sikhism stresses the importance of treating men and women equally. In order to show this equality, all Sikh men use the name 'Singh', meaning 'lion' and all Sikh women use the name 'Kaur', meaning 'princess'.

Sikhs also believe that if there is one God, then all people, from all religions, must be worshipping one God. Religious tolerance is very important. The Sikh Holy Scriptures, the **Guru Granth Sahib**, contains writings from teachers who were Hindus and Muslims.

**This is Guru Nanak, who founded Sikhism. The clothes he is wearing express his teachings about God and equality. He wears the yellow robe of a Hindu saint but also the turban and prayer beads of a Muslim.**

## ● THE MOOL MANTAR

Each section of the Guru Granth Sahib is introduced by a statement called the **Mool Mantar**. The Mool Mantar expresses the central beliefs about God. Here is an English translation.

> There is only one God,
> whose name is Truth.
> Who is the all-pervading Creator,
> without fear, without time,
> without form.
> Beyond birth and death,
> Self-enlightened.
> Known by the Grace of the Guru.

**Ik Onkar** is the first phrase of the Mool Mantar and means 'God is one'. It is a very widely used symbol in Sikhism and illustrates the importance of the belief in one God.

### THINK ABOUT IT!

1. Look at the picture of Guru Nanak. What do you think his clothes tell you about his beliefs about God and other religions?

**The Ik Onkar can be seen in many places, for example, on the walls of a gurdwara and in the home. It reminds Sikhs of their belief in one God.**

## IMAGES OF GOD

Sikhs believe that God has no form and so must never be pictured. There are, however, many names for God in the scriptures, and meditation upon the name of God is an important form of worship.

## THE TEN GURUS

There were nine gurus after Guru Nanak who led the Sikh community. Each one was chosen by his predecessor. Sikhs believe that God gave the gurus the ability to provide guidance and wisdom. Two gurus, Arjan and Teg Bahadur, were tortured to death by the ruling emperors because they taught and practiced religious freedom and tolerance. The tenth guru, Gobind Singh, taught that no other human would follow him as leader, instead the Sikhs were told to treat the holy scripture, the Guru Granth Sahib as their Guru.

Sikhs also make portraits of the ten gurus. The gurus are deliberately drawn to look alike. This is to show that, for Sikhs, what is important is not what the individuals might have looked like but the belief that they all carry the same spirit of the guru. You can imagine this to be like the way that a flame can be given from one candle to the next. There are different candles, but they all come from the same light.

## SERVICE TO GOD AND THE COMMUNITY

Sikhism teaches that the goal of life is to obey God's will. The gurus taught that service to God is shown through service to others. This is called **sewa**. Sikhs must therefore work in the community and ensure that everyone is helped and treated with justice. A good example of this is the way in which Sikh worship includes providing food from a kitchen run by volunteers. This is called **langar**.

The tenth Guru, Gobind Singh, taught that Sikhs who were devoted to their religion should wear five symbols to identify themselves. These include a **kirpan**, a sword whihc respresents dignity and respect and which shows Sikhs will fight to defend others if necessary.

### THINK ABOUT IT!

2. Belief in the equality of all people and the importance of helping others are central to Sikhism and follow on from the Sikh belief in one God. Set up a debate and choose one of these statements to support.
   **a)** 'If there is only one God then all religions must be worshipping the same God and so are equally important'
   **b)** 'Only one religion can be right about God, so all the others must be wrong'

   Give the reasons why you agree with one statement and disagree with the other.

### KEY WORDS

**Guru Granth Sahib** the holy book of Sikhism

**Mool Mantar** statement of belief at the beginning of the Guru Granth Sahib

**Ik Onkar** religious symbol in Sikhism expressing belief in one God

**Sewa** Sikh requirement to help others

**Langar** the kitchen and dining hall in a gurdwara and the food served in it

**Kirpan** one of the five K's, a sword

🎧 Why do you think the ten Gurus have been drawn to look alike? (Think back to what you have learned about symbolic art in chapter 2.)

In this lesson you will:
- examine Hindu beliefs about God
- design a symbol to represent something that is important to you
- look for and suggest meanings in Hindu symbols.

## 'THERE ARE MANY PATHS TO THE TRUTH'

This Hindu saying illustrates important ideas about Hindu belief. Hindus can have very different ideas from each other and worship in very different ways. There are, however, some beliefs about God that many Hindus share and you will explore some of these in this lesson.

## BRAHMAN

Most Hindus believe that there is one God, an underlying spirit, referred to as **Brahman**. They regard Brahman as the 'Ultimate Reality'. Everything is in Brahman and Brahman is in everything. Brahman is eternal and the source of all life.

Hinduism has hundreds of different deities that all represent Brahman (see Chapter 2, page 32–3). Three of the most important deities are Vishnu, Shiva and Durga.

Another significant deity is Krishna, a human form of Vishnu who came to earth to help humanity. Many Hindus offer worship and devotion to him and his female partner, Radha.

This is a statue of Shiva. It shows him performing the dance of life within the cycle of destruction and creation.

## THINK ABOUT IT!

1. Hindus use thousands of different deities to express the idea that the sacred is everything and in everything.
   a) Think of something that is important to you and draw an image or symbol to express it.
   b) Hindu deities are often associated with a particular animal. What animal would you choose to represent your idea and why?

## ● ONE OR MANY?

Non-Hindus are often confused by the idea that Hindus worship different deities and yet God is one. A Hindu would reply that humans are not able to imagine Brahman because Brahman is everything and so beyond human imagination. When Hindus want to show their love and devotion to God, they use images of deities.

These deities are all expressions of Brahman. Some Hindus explain this by using the example of the ocean. If you take a cup of water from it, that water is still part of the ocean although the rest of the ocean remains as vast as ever. In the same way, all the deities who are worshipped are like drops of water making up the great sea of Brahman.

## ● HOW DO HINDUS REPRESENT THE SACRED?

The sacred can be represented by living things. In some forms of Hindu worship, a flame represents the sacred and worshippers use purified butter or 'ghee' as an offering.

Hindus use many symbolic images and actions to show their devotion to God and their recognition of the sacred in all forms of life. One such symbolic action is the great respect and reverence shown to the cow.

The lotus flower is also often used in religious pictures. The lotus has its roots in the mud but its beautiful flower blossoms on the surface of the water. It illustrates the move away from the material world to be closer to God.

Another symbol for the sacred is the word Aum (sometimes spelt as Om). It represents the sound of God which brought the world into being (see chapter 2 page 31).

This is a picture of Krishna with his partner, Radha.

### THINK ABOUT IT!

2.  Make a list of reasons why Hindus might treat the cow as sacred. Here are some clues:
    ● most Hindus are vegetarians
    ● most Hindus in India live in small villages
    ● Hindus have great respect for motherhood.

### KEY WORDS

**Brahman** the supreme God in Hinduism, understood to be ultimate reality

# 3.8 ASSESSMENT ACTIVITY

## WHAT THIS TASK IS ALL ABOUT:

**1 a)** Choose two religions or worldviews that you feel you have a good knowledge of (for example, Christian, Muslim, Sikh, Hindu, Jew, Humanist, Atheist).

**b)** Now choose at least two key events from the list below. You are going to look at each event from the viewpoint of the religion you have chosen. You can use the same key events for each belief.

- The birth of a child
- A wedding
- A natural disaster
- The death of a close relative
- Taking the blame for somebody else
- Seeing a person being unfairly treated

**c)** For each religion, explain how a person might think and/or act in response to the events you have chosen and why they would respond in this way. For example:

*A Sikh might believe that if they see a person being treated unfairly, they should try to do something about it because one of their beliefs about God is that...*

## WHAT YOU NEED TO DO TO COMPLETE THE TASK:

For each viewpoint you need to explain:

- how a person might think/act
- how this might represent their views about God
- how that person's beliefs about God might influence them.

## HINTS AND TIPS

- Remember, do not be afraid to give your own opinion, but always give careful reasons for your ideas and show respect for the beliefs of other people.
- Your answers to this task will need to be from the viewpoint of at least two different beliefs.
- When choosing your religions, it may help you to cross out the religions that you do not want to use in your answers.
- You *can* use the same two key events for each of the beliefs you are looking at.
- Your written work should explain how a person from each of your chosen religions might think and/or act in response to the events you have chosen.
- In your answer, make sure you show that you understand the different views about God.
- Beliefs about God are often very personal, so you can only suggest how a person *might* react because of their beliefs.

| To ACHIEVE | You WILL NEED TO |
|---|---|
| Level 3 | Choose two different religions and explain how beliefs about God might affect the way a person would react to an event. |
| Level 4 | Choose at least two different religions and explain how beliefs about God might affect the way a person would react to an event. Discuss the views about God that would be important for each person and each event. |
| Level 5 | Choose at least two different religions and explain how beliefs about God might affect the way a person would react to an event. Discuss and explain the views about God that would be important for each person and each event. |
| Level 6 | Use a variety of religious beliefs to show how people's views about God influence the way that they think and act in response to key events. Show how and explain why people with different beliefs about God can approach the same events differently. |

# WHAT HAPPENS WHEN WE DIE?

# CHAPTER 4

## THE BIGGER PICTURE

Death has been said to be the only certainty in our lives. But it is also something we know very little about. There are many questions surrounding death. Do we enter into a different realm or do we return to live on earth again in the same form or different forms? Can belief in life after death affect the way we live our lives? These are the questions that this chapter explores.

### WHAT?

You will:
- investigate why people believe that there might be a life after death
- understand a variety of ideas about life after death
- reflect on the relationship between people's beliefs about life after death and the way they live their lives
- evaluate whether you think there could be a life after death and what really matters in this life.

### HOW?

By:
- studying examples of people's experiences that lead them to believe in a life after death
- reading accounts of what religious people believe can happen when they die
- making connections between beliefs in life after death and the way people live their lives
- looking at different viewpoints so you can form your own opinions on life after death and what is really important.

### WHY?

Because:
- you will understand what matters to people when someone dies and why their traditions and beliefs are important
- you need to consider how people's beliefs will change the way they regard life.

## KEY IDEAS

- Death is the one certain event faced by all human beings.
- All religions believe that death is not the end.
- Many religious people believe that the way they live affects what happens to them after they die.
- Whether we are religious or not our view of death has an impact on what we value in life.

## KEY WORDS

| | |
|---|---|
| Reincarnation | Gurmukh |
| Resurrection | Sewa |
| Gospel | Gurdwara |
| Akirah | Guru Granth Sahib |
| Allah | Nirvana |
| Karma | Samsara |
| Mukti | |

# WHY DO SOME PEOPLE BELIEVE IN LIFE AFTER DEATH?

In this lesson you will:
- investigate why people believe there might be a life after death
- consider whether near-death experiences and **reincarnation** are evidence for life after death
- reflect on how the Humanist view of life after death will affect Humanists' lives.

Near-death experiences often involve a bright light at the end of a tunnel

We do not know for certain what happens after we die. Here are two different experiences that some people use to support their belief that there is life after death: a near-death experience and reincarnation.

## IS THERE ANY EVIDENCE OF LIFE AFTER DEATH?

**Near-death experiences**

Some people say that when they have been pronounced dead and then been brought back to life, they have had an unusual experience. This is sometimes called a near-death, or out-of-body, experience. Read the account of a near-death experience below.

Some people believe that after death they will enter a beautiful garden and experience a happy and peaceful after-life.

**A**

'I was aware of being in the hospital bed. The next thing I knew, I was hovering above my body and looking down. Then I felt I was travelling at great speed down a black tunnel towards a brilliant white light.

I emerged from the light into a beautiful garden. It was heavenly and I felt joyful and happy. As I travelled along the path, I met up with my father who had died the previous year. He said I'd be very happy there and I knew he was right.

The next thing I knew, I was back in my body and the sensation of pain returned. It took me a long time to adjust. I wouldn't have described myself as 'religious' before, but now I feel that there is definitely a spiritual side to life and a life beyond death.'

Most near-death experiences include some of the elements mentioned above. A few people also mention having a sense of understanding or finding an answer that gives meaning and purpose to things that have happened. Others talk about having a review of their life when all the important experiences and moments flash before them.

## ● REINCARNATION

B

Reincarnation is the belief that when someone dies they return to life in another form. Some people feel very strongly that they are another person from a different time. One woman thought she was a child reincarnated because she remembered a time in India. Read the extract below to find out her thoughts on what happened.

'In 1935, a family in India, the Deva family, were worried about their daughter Shanti. At the age of three, she had begun to talk about a former life at a place called Muttra. Muttra is about 80 miles away from where the Devas lived. She said she had married a cloth merchant, had a son and died ten years later. At the age of nine, she was still claiming this to be the truth, so her family wrote to the man who was supposed to be her husband. He visited her home unannounced and was immediately recognized by Shanti. Shanti then went to Muttra and was able to find her way to the home, recognized who the relatives were and revealed that money had been hidden in the house. The hiding place was then found.'

## ● A HUMANIST VIEWPOINT

Humanists believe that this life is the only one we have. Death is the end.

Humanist beliefs are based on concern for others rather than belief in a god. We believe that humans should use their lifetime to build a better world, which will be just and caring. We believe that people should try to live full, happy lives and through their actions help others to achieve the same.

**Kerrie**

### KEY WORDS

**Reincarnation** the belief that after death a person's soul moves into another body and continues to live

## ? THINK ABOUT IT!

1. **a)** In small groups, write down five questions you would like to ask the people whose stories you have just read in A and B.
   **b)** Give your questions to another group. They must answer them from the point of view of each person on these pages.

2. How do you think a belief in reincarnation might affect how someone lives his or her life? Explain your answer.

3. What impact do you think the Humanist belief that there is no life after death might have on how Humanists might live their lives? Write a couple of sentences to show your thoughts.

4. Do you think that either experience A or B is evidence for life after death? Give reasons for your answer.

In this lesson you will:
- investigate why Christians believe in life after death
- examine one account of what happened to Jesus after his death
- analyse some explanations about what might have happened to Jesus' body and decide which you think is most likely.

## WHAT IS THE RESURRECTION?

Most Christians believe in a life after death because of the **resurrection** of Jesus. But what does this mean?

Christians believe that Jesus was raised from the dead and brought back to life by God after his crucifixion. This is an amazing claim and a central Christian belief.

For Mary Magdalene, Jesus was someone who had transformed her life and healed her, yet she had to watch him die on the cross, treated like a criminal.

According to the Bible, Jesus' body was taken down from the cross before sunset on the Friday. By morning, it had disappeared. John's **Gospel** describes what happened to Mary Magdalene that morning after she had found the empty tomb.

⟲ **What do you think this fifteenth-century painting says about the resurrection?**

'But Mary stood outside the tomb crying. As she wept, she bent over to look into the tomb and saw two angels in white, seated where Jesus' body had been, one at the head and the other at the foot. They asked her, 'Woman, why are you crying?'

'They have taken my Lord away,' she said, 'and I don't know where they have put him.'

At this, she turned round and saw Jesus standing there, but she did not realize that it was Jesus. 'Woman,' he said, 'why are you crying? Who is it you are looking for?'

Thinking he was the gardener, she said, 'Sir, if you have carried him away, tell me where you have put him.'

Jesus said to her, 'Mary.' She turned towards him and cried out in Aramaic, 'Rabboni!' (which means Teacher). '

*(John 20: 11–16)*

### KEY WORDS

**Resurrection** the belief that Jesus rose from the dead after his crucifixion. It can also mean a new life for Christians

**Gospel** the first four books of the New Testament: Matthew, Mark, Luke and John

## THINK ABOUT IT!

**1. a)** Work in pairs. Look up the following passages from the Bible that retell the story of what happened to Mary:

- Luke 8: 1–3
- Mark 15: 40–7
- John 20: 1–18.

**b)** Note down the key events from each passage. Next to each event, write down what you think Mary might have been thinking and feeling.

**2.** Now use what you have found to chart Mary's changing feelings and emotions on a graph. On the horizontal axis, list in order all the events you have looked at. On the vertical axis, list the emotions involved, starting with the most negative at the bottom and the most positive at the top.

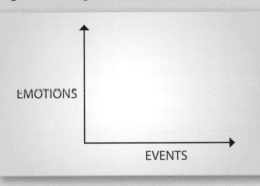

**3.** Use what you have discovered as the basis for a letter from Mary to a friend after Jesus' resurrection. In your letter, you need to tell your friend about Jesus, the impact he has had on your life and everything you have experienced.

## ● WHAT EVIDENCE IS THERE THAT JESUS REALLY DID RISE FROM THE DEAD?

Christians would argue that something extraordinary must have happened to Jesus to completely transform the lives of Mary Magdalene and the other disciples. Peter, one of the disciples, was later killed for his beliefs about Jesus.

In the next task, you will weigh up and sort out evidence for what happened to Jesus' body after he died.

## THINK ABOUT IT!

**4.** What happened to Jesus' body? How many theories you can come up with in answer to this question.

**5.** Be a detective! Read the passages below to find evidence for what happened to the body. What do you think is the best explanation for the missing body?

- Passages about the empty tomb: Matthew 27: 62–6; Mark 16: 1–8; Luke 24: 1–12; John 20: 1–10.
- Passages about Jesus' appearances after his death: Matthew 28: 1–15; Mark 16: 9–18; Luke 24: 13–49; John 20: 11–29; 1 Corinthians 15: 3–7.

In this lesson you will:
● investigate what Christians believe about life after death
● reflect on why Jesus' resurrection is important to Christians
● reflect on how the resurrection might affect people's lives today.

**B**elief in Jesus' resurrection is the foundation for Christians believing in life after death. Because they believe Jesus died and rose again, Christians believe that they, too, can have a new life after death. They believe that death is not the final part of life.

Before Jesus died, he told his followers:

**A**

'Do not let your hearts be troubled. Trust in God; trust also in me. In my Father's house are many rooms; if it were not so, I would have told you. I am going there to prepare a place for you.'

*(John 14: 1–2)*

**B**

'I am the resurrection and the life. He who believes in me will live, even though he dies.'

*(John 11: 25)*

## THINK ABOUT IT!

1. Choose either quote A or B and write a couple of sentences to explain what you think it means to Christians. Now pair up with someone else and tell them what you think the quote means.

## ● WHAT HAPPENS AFTER DEATH?

Christians believe that after death they will be judged on how they have responded to the teachings of Jesus in the way they live their lives and how they treat others. They believe that those who have lived a good life will go to heaven and those who have not will go to hell.

## ● WHAT DO CHRISTIANS BELIEVE ABOUT HELL?

Many Christians believe that hell is a state of being deparated from God. Some Christians picture it as a fiery place of punishment. The picture on this page shows this traditional view. This description was taken from Gehenna, a valley outside Jerusalem, where the city's rubbish was burned.

This is one artists' impression of the Christian view of life after death. What do you think is happening in each part of the picture?

## ● WHAT DO CHRISTIANS BELIEVE ABOUT HEAVEN?

For Christians, heaven is being where God is. It is a life of peace and happiness. They believe that life after death is a gift that God gives to those who believe and trust in Jesus.

Roman Catholic Christians also believe in purgatory. Purgatory is a place where people go after death before they enter heaven. In purgatory, they are purified so they are ready to be in God's presence.

### THINK ABOUT IT!

2. Draw a picture or write a description to show what you think a Christian would want heaven to be like.

3. 'Heaven is not a place, it's a state of mind'. Discuss in pairs.

🎧 **Some Christians believe that resurrection can be seen in the world today by bringing a change in people's lives. Here, aid is being brought to refugees.**

## ● HOW DOES THE RESURRECTION AFFECT CHRISTIANS' LIVES TODAY?

Christians often think of the resurrection in two ways.

- Firstly, it is the event when Jesus rose from the dead and gave hope to others that there is life after death.
- Secondly, it can be seen as a transformation, a dramatic change in someone's life. This could be when a criminal comes to believe in Jesus and realizes what they have done wrong. Or it could be on a much larger scale, where people are working to relieve poverty and suffering in poorer parts of the world.

### THINK ABOUT IT!

4. Look back at the people you have studied so far in this book. Note down the ones that you think show signs of a resurrection in their lives, along with the reason why you think that.

5. Can you think of any other people whose life has dramatically changed so they can follow their beliefs?

6. Why do you think that Jesus' resurrection is important to Christians today? Write a short paragraph to summarize your answer.

# 4.4 WHAT DO MUSLIMS BELIEVE ABOUT LIFE AFTER DEATH?

In this lesson you will:
- investigate what Muslims believe about life after death
- describe the impact of these beliefs on how a Muslim might live.

One of the central beliefs in Islam is belief in life after death, or **akirah** (see also Chapter 1, pages 14–15). Muslims do not believe that life ends when someone dies.

## ● JUDGEMENT

Islam means 'to submit'. Some might say that peace is achieved by doing what **Allah** wants. Therefore a Muslim is someone who submits to Allah. Muslims will aim to live good lives in order to serve Allah and worship him in their lives. Observing the Five Pillars of Islam is one way in which Muslims serve and worship Allah.

Muslims believe that after death two angels will take care of the soul until the Day of Judgement. On the Day of Judgement, the soul will be reunited with the body. The dead person will be asked, 'Who is your God? Who is your prophet? What is your religion?' The Day of Judgement is a time when everyone will be judged by Allah on what they have done in their lives and how they have served Allah.

### THINK ABOUT IT!

1. In pairs, make a list of the Five Pillars of Islam (see Chapter 1). Beside each one, note down one way in which Muslims can demonstrate this in their lives.

2. In your own words, explain why following the Five Pillars of Islam is important for Muslims.

## ● HEAVEN AND HELL

On the Day of Judgement, Muslims believe that those who have served Allah will be rewarded. Their sins will be forgiven and they will enter paradise or heaven. This is because Muslims believe that Allah is compassionate and merciful. Paradise is described as a beautiful garden.

They also believe that unbelievers will be punished and go to hell. Muslims believe that unbelievers have had a chance to turn to Allah during their lives but have rejected him. Hell is described as a scorching fire.

Muslims will regularly visit the graves of relatives to say prayers. They do this to remind themselves:

● that this life is short in comparison with eternal life
● that they must live in submission to Allah to please him and to ensure the rewards of paradise when they die.

### THINK ABOUT IT!

3. What effect do you think these beliefs in life after death will have on the way a Muslim lives his or her life?

4. What might a Muslim do to show their submission to Allah in their daily lives? (Refer back to Chapter 1 to help you answer this question.)

5. Muhammad said, 'When a person dies, the angels say, "What has he sent in advance?" But humans say, "What has he left behind?"' What do you think Muhammad meant?

### KEY WORDS

**Akirah**  Islamic belief in life after death

**Allah**  the Arabic name for God in Islam

◡ **Many Muslims believe that paradise will be like a beautiful garden.**

In this lesson you will:
- investigate what Sikhs believe about life after death
- reflect on how Sikh beliefs about life after death affect how Sikhs live their lives
- discuss your own views on what the purpose of life might be.

Read the following conversation. Ranjit, a thirteen-year-old Sikh, is explaining what Sikhs believe about life after death.

**Laura:** What do you believe about life after death?
**Ranjit:** We believe in reincarnation. We believe we will be reborn depending on our **karma**. Our karma is our actions and their consequences, the good and bad deeds we have done throughout our lives. When we die, our soul moves on to another body, so death is the opportunity for rebirth. If we live a good life and follow God's will, we can achieve **mukti**. This means escaping from the cycle of rebirth and achieving union with God.

**Laura:** What do you need to do to achieve mukti?
**Ranjit:** Sikhs believe that there is a spark of God in everyone. Sikhs want to please God and to become **gurmukh**, God-centred. If we act well during our life, then at the end, the spark will return to be united with God.

**Laura:** Are there any rules in Sikhism to help you live a good life?
**Ranjit:** Yes, we follow three basic rules: Nam Japna, Kirat karna and Vand chhakna.
- Nam Japna means remembering God and keeping God in mind by meditating.
- Kirat karna means earning your living in an honest way.
- Vand chhakna involves using your wealth, skills and time to help others.
All these things are a part of **sewa**.

**Laura:** What is sewa?
**Ranjit:** Sewa is about serving others. Sikhs believe that God is in everyone and by helping others you are serving God. There are three forms of sewa:
- tan is physical service, for example working in the langar or looking after the **gurdwara**
- man is mental service such as reading and studying the **Guru Granth Sahib**
- dhan is material service such as giving money or food, visiting the sick or caring for those in need.

**Laura:** So, what you are saying is that if you serve others, worship God, gain good karma and live a good life, you can be reunited with God?
**Ranjit:** Yes, we believe that this is our real purpose on earth.

**Laura:** What do you believe about the body that remains after death?
**Ranjit:** We believe that the body is simply clothing for the soul. When we die, we discard the body. Think of it like a butterfly emerging from the cocoon.

**Laura:** Are Sikh funerals in Britain very different to those in India?
**Ranjit:** Not really. In India, they probably happen within a day of death and there will be a funeral pyre near the sea or river lit by the eldest son, so they see the body burning.

**Laura:** Is it true that you do not have any headstones or memorials to remember the dead?

**Ranjit:** Yes. We are told that the best way to remember people is by their good deeds, not by looking at a stone.

**Laura:** If you had to sum up what you believe about death, what would you say?

**Ranjit:** I would quote from our holy book – the Adi Granth, which says: 'The dawn of a new day is the herald of a sunset. Earth is not our permanent home.'

⤴ **Sikhs believe that the soul leaves the body when they die, they imagine this to be like a butterfly emerging from a cocoon.**

## KEY WORDS

**Karma**  a teaching that states all actions will influence the next life

**Mukti**  the escape from rebirth

**Gurmukh**  someone who lives by the Gurus' teaching

**Sewa**  Sikh requirement to help others

**Gurdwara**  a Sikh place of worship

**Guru Granth Sahib**  the holy book of Sikhism

## THINK ABOUT IT!

1. What things do you think you should do to live a good life? How do these compare with what Sikhs believe?

2. The Japji Sahib is a prayer by Guru Nanak and the first chapter of the Guru Granth Sahib. These words are part of the Japji Sahib:

   '*We do not become saints or sinners by words or by saying that we are. It is our actions repeated over and over that are engraved on our soul. According to the seed we sow is the harvest that we shall reap. Nanak, by God's grace we are either released or reincarnated.*'

   Write a short paragraph to explain in your own words what this passage is saying and whether you agree with it or not.

3. What do you think Ranjit means when he says that Sikhs believe that the body is just clothing for the soul? Do you think this is a helpful idea? Give reasons for your answer.

4. What do you think the purpose of life is? Discuss your thoughts with a partner.

5. Create a presentation that shows the main Sikh beliefs about life after death.

In this lesson you will:
- explore what Buddhists believe about life after death
- reflect on the concept of **karma** and how this influences Buddhists' lives
- express your own opinions about karma and Buddhist beliefs about life after death.

## ● WHAT IS NIRVANA?

Most of the religions you have looked at so far teach a way of life that leads to God. Buddhism is different. The goal in Buddhism is to achieve **Nirvana**. Nirvana is not a place; it can be better described as a happy and contented state of mind.

Buddhism teaches that everyone has the ability to reach Enlightenment and Nirvana. The word 'Nirvana' means 'extinguished'. Buddhists believe that to achieve Nirvana they must extinguish the fires of greed, ignorance and hatred.

Achieving Nirvana can take many lifetimes and rebirths. Each life is an opportunity to escape from the cycle of births, illness, ageing, death and rebirth. This cycle is called **Samsara**.

The Buddha taught that one way to escape samsara was to follow the Noble Eightfold Path and to escape from wanting (see pages 18–19). When he gained Enlightenment, Buddha said, 'Having myself crossed the ocean of suffering, I must help others to cross it. Free myself, I must help others to be free.'

### KEY WORDS

**Nirvana**  point at which Enlightenment has been achieved

**Samsara**  the cycle of life: birth, illness, ageing, death and rebirth

### THINK ABOUT IT!

1. What do you think might stop someone achieving Nirvana?

2. a) What do you think people might desire today?
   b) Do you think fulfilling these wants will bring happiness?
   c) What do you think might bring a person true happiness?

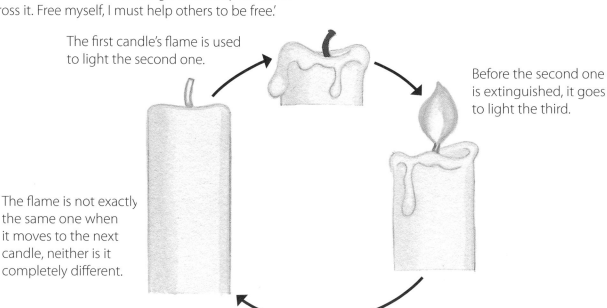

The first candle's flame is used to light the second one.

Before the second one is extinguished, it goes to light the third.

The flame is not exactly the same one when it moves to the next candle, neither is it completely different.

## ● 'AS YOU SOW, SO YOU WILL REAP'

Have you ever heard someone say this? It means that we get what we deserve in life. For example, if someone in your class does not bother to work hard, then they will probably not get the grades they are capable of achieving.

This is what **karma** means for Buddhists. Karma is like a law of cause and effect. If people do good, good will come to them, and if they do bad, bad will follow.

Buddhists believe that karma will go with someone into the next life. Try to imagine karma like a snooker ball. The karma is a force that passes from the snooker ball to the next ball it hits. When it touches the second ball, the first ball is stilled.

'All that we are is the result of our thoughts … If you speak or act with an evil thought, pain will follow you like the wheel that follows the ox that draws the wagon … If you speak or act with a pure thought, happiness will follow you like a shadow that never leaves you.'

*(Summary of the first two verses of the Dhammapada)*

**Buddhists believe that people are constantly changing physically, emotionally and mentally. People continually change during each lifetime as they aim to achieve Nirvana.**

### THINK ABOUT IT!

3. What do you think about the Buddhist idea of karma? Is it a fair way of explaining what happens in life?

4. Design a poster to illustrate the Buddhist beliefs you have learnt about in this lesson.

5. 'Buddhist teachings on life after death are really about how to live life in an effective way.' Do you agree? Give reasons for your answers.

# 4.7 ASSESSMENT ACTIVITY

## WHAT THIS TASK IS ALL ABOUT:

1 Choose two of the religions you have studied. Compare and contrast their beliefs about life after death.

2 Imagine you are a member of one of the religions you have chosen. Write a letter to a friend explaining how your beliefs about life after death affect your daily life. What does it teach you about the purpose of life?

3 Out of all the beliefs you have studied in this chapter, which one makes most sense to you? Explain your reasons.

## WHAT YOU NEED TO DO TO COMPLETE THE TASK:

- Look for the similarities and differences between the beliefs in the religions you have chosen.
- In your letter take each belief for the religion you have chosen and explain what difference it makes to your everyday life.
- Think about the differences your beliefs might make to how you treat others, how you spend your time and money.
- Think carefully about your own beliefs and ideas about what happens when we die and see if you can link them with the beliefs you have studied.

## HINTS AND TIPS

- Ensure that you give reasons to support what you say.
- Think carefully about how each religion's beliefs about death will affect the way believers live their lives.
- Decide on what you think happens after death and what you think is important about how you spend your time in this world.

| TO ACHIEVE | YOU WILL NEED TO |
|---|---|
| Level 3 | State some of the beliefs two different religions have about life after death and identify some things that are similar or different. Decide on one belief that you find most interesting and say why you think it is interesting. |
| Level 4 | Show some of the similarities and differences between what your chosen religions believe about life after death. You should discuss and explain clearly why you have chosen this belief system. |
| Level 5 | Develop the similarities and differences between the religions you have chosen by explaining clearly the beliefs and the important questions that they are trying to answer. Relate your chosen belief system clearly to your own life, drawing out what you feel is important. |
| Level 6 | Show what is special about each religion you have chosen as well as the similarities and differences between them, giving reasons for the differences. Explain not only how the beliefs help believers to come to terms with death but also how they affect your life. |

# CHAPTER 5

# BY WHAT AUTHORITY?

## THE BIGGER PICTURE

In this chapter you will be finding out about sources of authority. You will be investigating the qualities required by leaders, both religious and non-religious. You will also explore whether sacred writings and your own conscience can have authority.

### WHAT?

You will:
- investigate what it means to be in charge
- identify qualities a leader needs
- evaluate to what extent sacred writings have authority for religious believers
- investigate how we are all leaders.

### HOW?

By:
- discussing what leadership and authority mean
- comparing the leadership skills of different people
- considering the role of sacred writings as a source of authority for religious people
- considering your own leadership skills.

### WHY?

Because:
- many activities require leaders
- religions are often strongly influenced by people or sacred writings
- you need to consider how you lead yourself.

## KEY IDEAS

- Leaders have many important qualities.
- Religious leaders help people to follow the religion in the way they believe God wants them to.
- Religions also have books to provide leadership. They call these 'sacred writings'.
- Christianity has different types of leaders.
- Most leaders in Islam are called an imam.
- The first Jewish king (Saul) took over leadership of the Jews from God.
- Sikhs turn to their sacred book, the Guru Granth Sahib, as a source of authority.
- Individual people have to lead themselves.
- Religious beliefs have affected the laws in most countries, including Britain.

## KEY WORDS

| | |
|---|---|
| Leadership | Pope |
| Responsibility | Moral |
| Authority | Vicar |
| Qur'an | Imam |
| Allah | Archbishop |
| Bishop | Protestant |
| Charisma | Vocation |
| Gospels | Guru |
| Guru Granth Sahib | Gurdwara |
| Langar | Granthi |
| Conscience | Moral code |

Love your enemies and pray for those who do you wrong.

Vote for me!

Nobody is going to tell me what to do.

In this lesson you will:
- decide on the qualities needed by leaders
- reflect on your own **leadership** qualities
- evaluate the qualities the **Pope** possesses.

**The Prime Minister is elected to be in charge of the country.**

**H**ave you ever thought about how people become leaders? Sometimes leaders are chosen by others, perhaps in an election. Sometimes they take the position for themselves, often against the wishes of others. However they become a leader, they must have qualities to do the job well.

The qualities they need depend on the type of leader they are going to be. It is not necessary for a prime minister to be good at football; but for the captain of a football team it is essential. The manager of a factory does not need the same qualities as the manager of a sweet shop.

One thing that most leaders have in common is that they are in charge of other people and they have a **responsibility** for those people. This means that they should not abuse or harm them. To be a responsible leader they must care for, help, guide and respect those they lead.

One good leader is worth a hundred willing followers.

**anon**

## ? THINK ABOUT IT!

**1. a)** Make a list of the qualities that you think the following leaders need to have:
  - a prime minister
  - a football captain.

  **b)** How are these qualities similar and how are they different?

  **c)** Highlight the top three qualities that you think each leader needs to do his or her job well. Explain your choices.

  **d)** Compare your choices with a partner or in small groups.

## ● WHO IS IN CHARGE OF YOUR SCHOOL?

Think about your school.
- The leaders are the governors and the head teacher, possibly helped by a deputy head and a small team of senior teachers or assistant heads.
- Each department or faculty is led by a subject leader who is in charge of the teachers in that department or faculty.
- You might have heads of year or heads of house who are in charge of a group of pupils.
- Your teachers are in charge of leading your learning so they must show the sorts of qualities that good leaders have.
- You may have prefects at school who help teachers by setting a good example.

### KEY WORDS

**Leadership** the role of leading a person or group

**Pope** the head of the Roman Catholic Church

**Responsibility** looking after, managing, taking the blame on behalf of others

**Moral** the correct way to behave

**Authority** the power or right to be a leader of others

## THINK ABOUT IT!

**2.** Make a table like the one below showing the leaders of your school. For each leader, add one quality that you think is important for them to do their job well.

| Title | Name | Quality |
|---|---|---|
| Head teacher | | |
| Deputy or assistant head | | |
| Head of department or faculty | | |
| Head of year or house | | |
| RE teacher | | |
| Me | | |

## ● BEING A LEADER

Perhaps you are a leader yourself. You might be the captain of a sports team or be on the school council. You might be a role model at home for your younger brothers and sisters.

## THINK ABOUT IT!

**3.** Note down the ways in which you think you are a leader.

**4.** Add to your notes the qualities that you need to be a successful leader.

## ● RELIGIOUS LEADERS

Religions have leaders, too. There is often a person who has overall charge of a religion.

The Roman Catholic Church is led by the Pope. Roman Catholic Christians believe that God has chosen the Pope to be their leader. The Pope governs the Roman Catholic Church and looks after its followers. He has various duties and responsibilities.

- Roman Catholics believe that when speaking on **moral** or religious matters, as Jesus' representative on earth, the Pope cannot be wrong. This is called Papal infallibility.

- The Pope has the power to discipline individual Roman Catholics who do wrong, including being able to excommunicate them (exclude them from the Church).

- The Pope must also forgive people on behalf of God.

The Pope has great **authority** and many Roman Catholics believe that what he says about religious or moral issues is very important.

## THINK ABOUT IT!

**5.** 'The Pope's most important quality is that he must be very caring.' Give two arguments in favour of this statement and two arguments against. (You might want to think of a more important quality to help with your arguments against.) Which do you agree with most?

In this lesson you will:
- reflect on whether religious leaders have authority from God
- understand the leadership structure of the Church
- evaluate the role of a religious leader.

🎧 **Can you identify any of the religious leaders in these photographs? How many other religious leaders can you think of?**

In the last lesson we looked at the qualities leaders need. We found that a leader has a responsibility to care for the people he or she leads and that they should have authority in order to be successful. This also applies if someone is leading a religion or a group of religious people.

## ● LEADERS OF RELIGION

Many religious people expect their leaders to have more of God's qualities than other non-religious leaders. If they go to their religious leader for help or advice, they might expect the answer to be like the one they believe God would give them.

Many Christians believe that God gives their leaders special powers when they become priests or **vicars**, and this gives them more authority than someone who is not a priest or vicar.

Muslims choose their leader, who they call an **imam**, from men who have learnt a lot about the **Qur'an** or Holy Book. Their wisdom comes from the Qur'an, which they believe is the word of **Allah**.

## ● CHRISTIAN LEADERS

### THE ROMAN CATHOLIC CHURCH

In the last lesson, we found out that the leader of the Roman Catholic Church is called the Pope.

The Pope is chosen by a group of people called cardinals and anybody who is not a cardinal cannot become Pope.

Underneath the cardinals are **bishops**, who oversee the running of several churches in one area.

Underneath the bishops are priests, who are responsible for a local church or community.

### THE CHURCH OF ENGLAND

The Church of England is the largest **Protestant** Church in Britain.

The head of the Church of England is the monarch, who takes the title 'Defender of the Faith'.

There are two **archbishops** who lead the Church on behalf of the monarch. The most important of these is the Archbishop of Canterbury.

Underneath the archbishops are bishops, who are responsible for several churches in one area.

The bishops are supported by archdeacons from their area.

Underneath the archdeacons are priests or vicars, who are responsible for a local church or community.

Other Christian denominations have similar leadership structures to make sure the help and guidance religious people need is there for them from people they can trust.

## ● WHAT DO RELIGIOUS LEADERS DO?

Religious leaders lead worship. They will hold services, when people come together to worship, and are in charge of what goes on at a service of worship. They are available to help people in need at any time and are expected to become involved in local events.

> Sorry, I can't help you. I have prayers to lead.

### THINK ABOUT IT!

1. What do you think about what the priest is saying? Explain your answer, thinking carefully about what you know about the duties that a religious leader has.

Sometimes a religious leader may decide to become involved in sorting out something they feel is a serious problem. This may be a religious issue, but often it will be a moral or social issue about how people live their day-to-day lives. For example, they may become involved in projects to relieve poverty or to try to end racism.

Whatever they do, religious leaders are expected to be good role models. This means they are expected to set a good example for other people to follow.

### KEY WORDS

**Vicar** a Christian leader in charge of worship in a parish

**Qur'an** the holy book of Islam

**Imam** a leader of prayer in Islam

**Allah** the Arabic name for God in Islam

**Archbishop** one of the most important leaders in Christianity

**Bishop** a Christian leader

**Protestant** a part of the Christian church different from the Roman Catholic and Orthodox churches

### THINK ABOUT IT!

2. Draw a spider diagram with the title of a religious leader in the middle.
   a) With a partner, try to include six special things you think a religious leader does.
   b) Now rank these special things in order of importance by numbering them.
   c) Give reasons for why you have selected your order of importance.

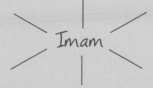

Imam

3. Think about the world today. What things do you think a religious leader should be concerned about? Give reasons for the issues you have selected.

In this lesson you will:
- analyse the importance of one aspect of leadership: **charisma**
- reflect on the idea that God might actively help people in their work
- express individual ideas about charisma and **vocation**.

In 2005, a famous French footballer advertised Renault cars by referring to their 'va va voom'. The manufacturer wanted to identify an extra special something about their cars that made them stand out from the rest, but that was hard to put into words.

The French also use the phrase 'je ne sais quoi' to describe something not easily described. Perhaps this 'je ne sais quoi' or 'X factor' is what makes one person a 'pop idol' and leaves the rest as merely singers.

Do you think that Thierry Henry has Va Va Voom? How can you tell?

## WHAT IS CHARISMA?

Many leaders possess a quality that makes them very different from other people. It is as if they have some extra va va voom! This is sometimes defined as their charisma.

Not all religious leaders, political leaders, sports stars or pop stars are charismatic, but some are. They stand out from the crowd and are seen as special.

So what is charisma? It can be defined as a natural or God-given power that some people have to influence or attract people. Whilst this is helpful, it does not tell us any information about what this special power is like. Perhaps it is one of those words that we cannot define but which we can recognize when we see it in someone.

**THINK ABOUT IT!**

1. Name a person who you think has charisma. Why do you think they have charisma?

2. Write a short paragraph to describe how having charisma helps this person.

## ● WHAT DOES IT MEAN TO HAVE A VOCATION?

Many people believe that they have been inspired to follow a certain career. This is called having a **vocation**. This calling does not just apply to people who become leaders. Many people see nursing or working for the emergency services as vocations, some even see teaching in this way.

Some religious people with a vocation feel that it is God who has inspired them, who gives them the skills to do their work and supports them whilst they are doing it.

Whatever the vocation is, it usually involves helping other people and being responsible for them in the same way that a leader has responsibility for those he or she leads.

**THINK ABOUT IT!**

3.  a)  Write down three questions that you would like to ask a nurse about their work; for example, why he or she chose that career, does he or she believe they have a vocation? If so, what or who inspired them?

    b)  Choose somebody to go in the hotseat. They must pretend to be a nurse. In turns, ask your questions.

4.  Some people believe that God inspires them to do a certain job and supports them in doing it. In pairs, discuss whether or not you think this is possible. Give reasons for your answer and be prepared to share your ideas with the class.

# 5.4 BORN TO BE KING?

In this lesson you will:
- investigate the events in the life of King Saul
- identify the qualities shown by King Saul
- reflect on the concept of a leader chosen by God.

Most kings and queens inherit their position when the previous king or queen dies. They are not chosen by anybody and it is possible that they do not have the qualities they need to lead a country. This will not prevent them from taking the job because they are born into it.

## ● WE WANT A KING!

Over 3000 years ago, the Hebrews (the ancient Jews) were ruled by judges. The prophet Samuel was one of these judges. Samuel had been chosen by God from an early age and possessed great authority:

> 'The Lord continued to appear at Shiloh, where he had appeared to Samuel and had spoken to him.'
>
> *(1 Samuel 3: 21)*

Samuel had authority over the judges. This might have been because he continued to believe in God when most of the others did not.

One day, leaders chosen by the people suggested to Samuel that they should have a king who would rule them and lead them in battle. Samuel was disappointed because he believed that God was their king. The people ignored Samuel's advice and insisted that they should have a king. After much prayer, God told Samuel that he should appoint a king.

Elizabeth II was born into the Royal Family and became Queen following the abdication of Edward VIII and the death of her father

## THINK ABOUT IT!

1. Think of a leader you know about. How did they become leader?

2. Once God agreed, how do you think Samuel should have chosen a king? Should he have made the decision himself or left it up to God or to the Hebrews themselves?

# WHO WAS KING SAUL?

Saul was a handsome man who became the first king of the Hebrews in Israel. He was also the tallest man amongst the Hebrews. Kish, Saul's father, was a wealthy man who had a great influence over people. It seems he brought Saul up very well.

One day, Kish asked Saul to take a servant with him to look for two donkeys that had wandered off. After several days of searching, Saul suggested going back home in case his father was worried. The servant persuaded Saul to ask Samuel for help in finding the donkeys.

Unknown to Saul, God had told Samuel that Saul would come to see him and that he should anoint Saul as the new king.

Samuel did as God told him and then called the people together. He introduced Saul as their new king, stressing that he was God's choice. Most people were happy but some were unhappy because they didn't feel Saul would be a good leader.

Over the years, Saul won many battles against the enemies of Israel. However, he disobeyed God, so God disowned him and asked Samuel to anoint the next king – King David. David was not king straight away because, although God had disowned him, Saul continued in the job. Saul tried to have David killed because he was jealous but he failed each time.

David eventually became king when Saul committed suicide in a battle.

You can read the story of Saul in the Old Testament of the Bible, in 1 Samuel 8—10.

🎧 **Samuel anointing Saul**

## THINK ABOUT IT!

3.  **a)** Make a list of six key words that tell us about what sort of man Saul was and what he looked like.

    **b)** Give each of these key words a mark out of 5 to show how important you think they are for a successful king (0 = unimportant; 5 = essential). Explain why you have chosen your most and least important key word.

4.  Do you think it is important for a king or queen to believe in God? Say why or why not.

In this lesson you will:
- reflect on the idea of God's authority being shown through sacred writings
- understand that people's lives are influenced by sacred writings.

## ● WHY WRITE SOMETHING DOWN?

In the 1970s, a woman called Kim Casali devised a series of cartoons to show her feelings for her husband. They have become known as the 'Love is ...' cartoons and were usually quite romantic.

The cartoons proved to be a good way of getting a message across. For some people, something written or printed holds more authority than something that is said. Spoken words disappear as soon as they are said, whereas written words can exist and be treasured forever. The 'Love is ...' cartoons are permanent reminders of Kim's love for her husband.

**THINK ABOUT IT!**

1. Think of a caption for your own 'Love is ...' cartoon. You do not have to draw the cartoon. Now do the same for a 'Love is not ...' cartoon.

◡ **Love is... never having to say sorry.**

BILL ASPREY.

## ● WHAT ARE SACRED WRITINGS?

All religions have beliefs and teachings that believers consider important. These beliefs and teachings are often recorded in sacred writings. The importance of these sacred writings often comes from the belief that God or a higher power had some part in them being written. In this lesson you will find out about why the sacred writings of Christianity and Islam are respected and are believed to hold authority.

**THINK ABOUT IT!**

2. In pairs, name as many sacred writings as you can. Then identify which religion they come from.

## ● SACRED WRITINGS IN CHRISTIANITY

Many Christians believe that the four **Gospels** in the Bible contain the words of Jesus, written by four men who were writing for and on behalf of God. Many believe that the writings have great authority because the writers record what they or other people actually saw and heard during Jesus' lifetime. Many even believe that God inspired the writers.

However, one of the most famous Christian passages in the New Testament was not written by Matthew, Mark, Luke or John, but by Paul in 1 Corinthians 13. Christians believe that Paul was guided and inspired by God from the moment he became a Christian, right through to his death. This includes his writings, which is what makes them especially important to Christians.

The passage is about love and often read during a Christian marriage ceremony. Its ideas have more depth than the 'Love is …' cartoons and it is not just about romantic love. You may want to read it for yourself. It says that:

| Love is … | Love is not … |
| --- | --- |
| Patient | Jealous |
| Kind | Conceited |
| Happy with the truth | Proud |
| Eternal | Ill-mannered |
| Greater than faith and hope | Selfish |
| | Irritable |
| | Happy with evil |

### THINK ABOUT IT!

3. Copy the 'Love is …/Love is not …' table above. In a different colour, add any other words you think should be there. Be prepared to talk about the words you have added and why.

### KEY WORDS

**Gospel** the first four books of the New Testament: Matthew, Mark, Luke and John

## ● SACRED WRITINGS IN ISLAM

Muslims believe that their sacred writings in the Qur'an are the actual words of Allah as given to the Prophet Muhammad. They believe that the Qur'an was revealed to Muhammad by the angel Jibril over a period of 20 years. This makes the Qur'an very important. Muslims believe that it is Allah's way of permanently communicating with His people. For this reason, the Qur'an is never changed and is usually read in the original Arabic language.

Muslims also follow the advice given in the Hadiths. These are a collection of teachings and sayings from Muhammad. Muslims respect the Hadiths because they believe that Muhammad is a good example to follow. They will often turn to the Hadiths for guidance.

The Qu'ran is treated with respect. Muslims must not speak, eat or drink while reading it.

### THINK ABOUT IT!

4. Why do you think religious people trust what their sacred books tell them? Think of three reasons.

5. What problems might there be in relying on sacred writings?

In this lesson you will:
- identify the importance of the **Guru Granth Sahib** for Sikhs
- evaluate the Sikh view of the unchanging nature and authority of the Guru Granth Sahib.

Imagine that you are the captain of the Year 6 football team. You are moving to secondary school but you care about the progress the team is going to make without you. Given the chance, you might want to choose somebody you trust to take over captaincy of the team. The problem is that you are worried that the person you choose might make some tactical changes you would not approve of. Over time, all these little changes, when added up, may make things very different from your original ideas.

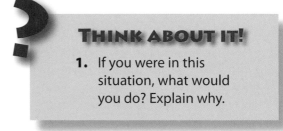

### THINK ABOUT IT!

1. If you were in this situation, what would you do? Explain why.

Guru Gobind Singh, the tenth Sikh **guru**, faced a similar problem. Before his time there had been nine other gurus or leaders who helped to spread the new ideas and religion of the first guru – Guru Nanak. They had tried not to change Guru Nanak's ideas and teachings but some differences did creep in.

### ● NO MORE HUMAN GURUS

In order to stop future gurus from changing the ideas and teachings of Sikhism, Guru Gobind Singh decided to declare the sacred writings of Sikhism, called the Adi Granth, the final and permanent guru.

Guru Gobind Singh called the Adi Granth the Guru Granth Sahib. He said that this would be important to us because Guru Nanak and the other gurus wrote it. It has not changed since then. I have even seen the original copy when I visited India last year. It was awesome!

**Ranjit**

🎧 **Guru Gobind Singh was the last human guru. He declared that the Guru Granth Sahib would be the final Guru.**

## ● WHAT ABOUT TODAY?

The Guru Granth Sahib is still regarded as the final authority for Sikhs today. There is a copy of it as a focal point in every **gurdwara** from where it is read aloud. It is treated with great respect.

- It is placed on a throne called a manji sahib.
- When it is open, there will always be a Sikh sitting with it.
- People wash and remove their shoes before they enter the gurdwara as a mark of respect. They must cover their heads.

- Sikhs make offerings of money or food before the Guru Granth Sahib. These are used by the **langar**, a kitchen which provides a meal for everybody in the gurdwara.
- At night, it is put to rest.

If Sikhs need advice, they will get it from the Guru Granth Sahib, possibly with the help of a **granthi**. Anybody who can read is able to be a granthi.

Look at the photo below. How do you think it shows respect being shown to the Guru Granth Sahib?

### KEY WORDS

**Guru Granth Sahib** the holy book of Sikhism

**Guru** a religious teacher in Sikhism and Hinduism

**Gurdwara** a Sikh place of worship

**Langar** kitchen and dining hall in a gurdwara and the food served

**Granthl** reader of the Guru Granth Sahib who leads cermonies in Sikhism

The Guru Granth Sahib is written in Punjabi. Every copy is exactly the same and has 1430 pages.

### THINK ABOUT IT!

2. Why do you think Sikhs show respect to the Guru Granth Sahib? How do you think the ways listed show respect?

3. a) What do you think are the advantages and disadvantages of following the teaching of: **i)** a person, and **ii)** a book?

   b) Which would you be more likely to trust and why? Write a short summary of your thoughts.

4. Do you think the fact that the Guru Granth Sahib has not been changed from the original makes it more or less worth reading? Give two reasons to support your opinion and one reason against it.

In this lesson you will:
- find out what **conscience** is and where it might come from
- investigate the effect of conscience on our actions
- discuss whether conscience is useful and God-given.

One of the characteristics of being human is that we can choose what we do. This is called free will. If we do something good, we feel pleased with ourselves, but if we do something wrong, then we do not! This is known as 'having a conscience'.

Part of having free will is being able to choose our own set of rules to live by. This set of rules is sometimes called a **moral code**. For many people, but not for all, a moral code is attached to a religion.

However, it is quite common for a non-religious person's moral code to be similar to a religious person's. Why is this?

Read the Ten Commandments below. How many do you agree with? Even though this is a religious code, few people would argue with the commandments 'do not commit murder' or 'do not steal'. The fact that they are religious does not rule them out for non-religious people.

## THE TEN COMMANDMENTS

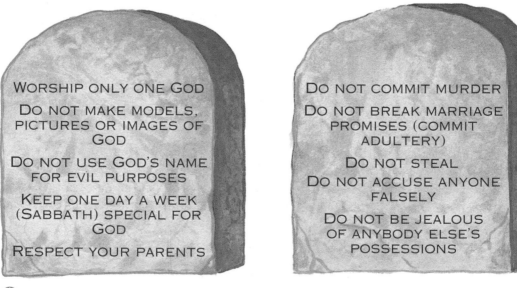

WORSHIP ONLY ONE GOD

DO NOT MAKE MODELS, PICTURES OR IMAGES OF GOD

DO NOT USE GOD'S NAME FOR EVIL PURPOSES

KEEP ONE DAY A WEEK (SABBATH) SPECIAL FOR GOD

RESPECT YOUR PARENTS

DO NOT COMMIT MURDER

DO NOT BREAK MARRIAGE PROMISES (COMMIT ADULTERY)

DO NOT STEAL

DO NOT ACCUSE ANYONE FALSELY

DO NOT BE JEALOUS OF ANYBODY ELSE'S POSSESSIONS

🎧 **The Ten Commandments, respected by Jews and Christians, make up one of the most well-known moral codes.**

## ? THINK ABOUT IT!

1. **a)** Does your own moral code allow you to do the following?
   - Tell lies all the time.
   - Tell lies in certain circumstances.
   - Steal because you want something you cannot afford.
   - Disrespect your parents because they are getting on your nerves.
   **b)** Compare your answers with a partner. Decide why each one is the same or different.

## ● WHY HAVE A MORAL CODE?

Religious people believe that they have an incentive to follow a moral code and the teachings of their religion. Many believe that they will spend eternity with God or be reincarnated at a higher level if they follow the teachings of their religion.

However, many people who do not follow a religion or who do not believe in God also live their lives by a moral code. Read what a Humanist might say in the speech bubble on the right.

> As a Humanist, I follow certain rules to ensure that I do not harm other people. I believe we all have the right not to be harmed purely by the fact that we are human beings.

**Kerrie**

### THINK ABOUT IT!

2. Think of a time when you did something good. How did you feel when you had done it?

3. Think of a time when you did something bad. How did you feel when you had done it?

---

### KEY WORDS

**Conscience**  how people decide what is right and wrong

**Moral code**  a set of rules that help people decide the right thing to do

---

## ● YOU AND YOUR CONSCIENCE

Your answer to question 3 will probably include some uncomfortable or unpleasant feelings! Some people think that such feelings are helpful because they stop us doing something bad in the future. They call this feeling our 'conscience'.

It is sometimes said that somebody who does something especially bad, for example commits murder, does not have a conscience. If they had, they would not have committed such a horrible crime.

Some religious people believe that God created people with a conscience so that they will do as He taught them. Humanists and others who do not believe in God might argue that conscience is connected to how humans have evolved or have been brought up.

> I wish I didn't have a conscience – I feel bad too often

### THINK ABOUT IT!

4. Explain what the word 'conscience' means to you.

5. Do you think your conscience has anything to do with God? Attempt your answer in writing first and then discuss it with a partner.

 **Do you think that criminals can have a conscience?**

### WHAT THIS TASK IS ALL ABOUT:

1 Make a list of the qualities you would expect a religious leader to possess. Choose three of these qualities and explain carefully why they are helpful to a religious leader. Use examples of leaders as illustrations of these qualities.

2 Script an interview with one of the people you have studied in this chapter (the Pope, King Saul or Guru Gobind Singh). Include questions about what they have done in their life and why they did them. Finish your interview with a summary of why you think your chosen person is important for religious believers.

3 Create a presentation about one of the sacred writings you have studied, including some of the teachings it contains and its importance for religious believers. Your presentation should summarize the key issues and include an introduction (two slides), development of your argument (up to six slides) and a conclusion (two slides).

### WHAT YOU NEED TO DO TO COMPLETE THE TASK:

- Try to show how your leader/sacred writings lead/have led people.
- Include some of the qualities your leader/sacred writings possess.
- Explain why you hold any opinion you choose to write.
- Think about reasons why people may disagree with your ideas and opinions. Include these reasons as well as your own.

### HINTS AND TIPS

- Make sure you include enough detail.
- If you are asked for an opinion, you should give your reasons as well.
- Once you have given your reasons, try to think of a different opinion from your own and give reasons for that different opinion as well.
- Try to show how the beliefs of a religion affect what a person thinks or does.

Love your enemies and pray for those who do you wrong.

| TO ACHIEVE | YOU WILL NEED TO |
| --- | --- |
| Level 3 | Describe the importance of beliefs and teachings for religious believers. Identify how these beliefs and teachings influence how people decide to behave. |
| Level 4 | Show that you understand the experiences of a religious person and the importance of beliefs and teachings for religious believers. Use your own experience and ideas about religious beliefs to show why people behaved/behave the way they did or do. Apply your ideas about religious beliefs and teachings to people's lives. |
| Level 5 | Explain the experiences of a religious person and the importance of beliefs and teachings for religious believers. Express your own views about how religious beliefs and teachings make a difference to people's lives and the life of the community. |
| Level 6 | Explain the experiences of a religious person and the importance of beliefs and teachings for religious believers. Express opinions about and insights into the teachings and experiences of inspirational religious people and relate these to your own life and the lives of others. |

Vote for me!

VOTE

Nobody is going to tell me what to do.

# CHAPTER 6

# WHAT DOES IT MEAN TO BE HUMAN?

## THE BIGGER PICTURE

In this chapter you will look at whether human beings are different from all the other creatures in the animal kingdom, and if they are, then why? You will explore the idea that there is something more to human beings than meets the eye, something more than the physical, something perhaps that we cannot see or point to, or maybe even describe.

## WHAT?

You will:
- explore the ways in which people suggest that humans are special and unique
- reflect upon ideas about the soul
- enquire into the nature of ultimate questions- important questions that have no definite right or wrong answer and which cannot be proved
- evaluate the idea that it is humans' ability to ask and try to answer complex questions that makes them unique.

## HOW?

By:
- exploring and suggesting your own ideas about what makes humans different from other creatures
- investigating different beliefs about the soul and what might happen when people die
- showing that you can use your learning about symbolic stories to decode the hidden meanings in religious texts
- thinking of your own ultimate questions.

## WHY?

Because:
- some people might hold ideas that are different to your own
- you need to be able to empathize with those ideas and be respectful of them, even if you disagree
- thinking of your own ultimate questions about existence will help you appreciate the thoughts of others.

# KEY IDEAS

- Human beings are very different from other creatures.
- Many people are religious and have different ideas about what happens when they die.
- Different religions have different ideas about whether humans have a soul.
- Human beings ask themselves 'ultimate' questions. Is it this that makes them unique compared to other animals?
- Human beings have certain rights What is it about being human that means people should have these rights? And do all humans feel as though they are indeed protected by these rights?

# KEY WORDS

| | |
|---|---|
| Philosophers | Conscience |
| Soul | Morality |
| Spiritual | Allah |
| Samsara | Nirvana |
| Reborn | Karma |
| Symbolic | Neanderthal |
| Shoah | Stewardship |

🎧 'What makes humans unique?'

In this lesson you will:
- explore the differences between humans and the rest of the animal kingdom
- reflect upon and evaluate what makes humans unique.

Have you ever wondered why your hair keeps growing? Or why, when you cut yourself, the skin can heal itself? The human body is an amazing machine!

Just take your lungs, for example.
- Did you know that if you spread all the alveoli (the little air sacks inside your lungs) out flat, they would have the same surface area as a tennis court!
- If you spread out all the capillaries (blood vessels) in your lungs end to end, they would stretch from London to New York. That is about 3000 miles!

And what about the brain? You have over 100 billion (100,000,000,000,000) nerve cells in your brain. These cells allow you to remember 1 million pieces of data, including over 100,000 words. They even allow you to recognize over 2000 faces!

However, this is not what makes humans unique.

A chimpanzee's genetic make-up (DNA) is 99 per cent similar to a human. Some chimpanzees can manufacture and use basic tools, and all are able to communicate with each other in highly complex ways.

A dolphin's brain contains almost as many nerve cells as a human's and recent research suggests they can even recognize themselves in mirrors, indicating that they have a sense of their own existence.

### KEY WORDS

**Philosophers** great thinkers who try to understand the meaning of life

**Conscience** how people decide what is right or wrong

**Soul** the spiritual or emotional centre of a person said to survive death

**Morality** behaving in a way that fits with your moral code and conscience

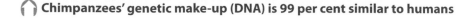
**Chimpanzees' genetic make-up (DNA) is 99 per cent similar to humans**

## ● WHAT MAKES YOU, YOU?

Have you ever sat and wondered what makes you, you?

What makes humans different from all the other animals in the world?

Are humans actually any different?

These are questions that scientists, **philosophers**, religious people, and many others have been thinking about for centuries. So what answers have they come up with? What answers would you come up with?

These are tricky questions to answer. In fact, there may be no right or wrong answers at all, just opinions that cannot be proved either way. However, the fact that we can even try to answer them might be another reason why we are unique. Humans are the only creatures that wonder why they exist and then attempt the impressive task of finding out.

🎧 **Is every human being in this crowd unique?**

## THINK ABOUT IT!

1.  What are the main differences between humans and other animals?
    a)  Look at the following list of words. Draw a table similar to the one below and sort the words into the three categories. Can some of the words fit in more than one column?

| Human | Animal | Not sure |
|---|---|---|
|  |  |  |

   Emotions, **conscience**, body, personality, **soul**, religious belief, intelligence, brain, language, **morality**, communication

    b)  Now add more words to your 'Human' list. What else is unique to humans? Think about your own life and experiences, and those of the people around you.

    c)  Using the words you put in the 'Human' column write a paragraph to explain your ideas about what makes humans unique.

2.  'What makes humans unique?' One man who tried to answer this was a philosopher called Rene Descartes (1596–1650). He famously wrote, 'I think, therefore I am!'

    a)  What do you think he meant by this?
    b)  What do you think of his view?
    c)  Swap your answers with a partner and discuss each other's ideas – how are they different? Have you thought of similar reasons? Have you both explained your opinions and given reasons for your answers?

In this lesson you will:
- enquire into Christian and Muslim beliefs about the soul
- evaluate whether having a soul is what makes humans unique
- reflect upon whether people must believe in a God in order to believe that they have a soul.

## WHAT IS 'THE SOUL'?

- If you were asked to point to your mind, where would you place your finger?
- If you were asked to point to your heart, where would you place your finger?
- If you were asked to point to your self, where would you place your finger?

If you were pointing to your head, you would be pointing to your brain, about 1.5 kg of blood and nerve cells. If you were pointing to your chest, you would be indicating your heart, which is a muscular pump about the same size as your fist. So, where is your 'self'?

Some scientists would argue that we are nothing but a complex mix of chemicals, that make up bones, muscles and organs. However, other people, both religious and non-religious, believe that human beings are more than just a physical body. They might refer to the spirit, mind, self or soul. Some people argue that it is the existence of the soul that makes humans unique. Our soul is 'our self'.

### THINK ABOUT IT!

1. What does the word 'soul' mean to you?

2. If the soul exists, what do you think the point of it might be?

## THE SOUL IN CHRISTIANITY

Many Christians believe that humans have a **spiritual** element to them that makes them special and sets them apart from all other animals. They believe that spiritual element is not a physical part of the body. Some people might suggest that this spiritual aspect could be thought of as a soul. Christians believe that humans are created 'in God's image' and that this spirit or soul is a reflection of this image inside every person.

In Christianity, it is believed that the spirit enables humans to communicate with God through prayer and worship. Some say that if they believe in Jesus and ask for his forgiveness for their sins, then their spirit will be saved and they will go to heaven when they die.

Many people believe that when we die our soul carries on living in the world as a ghost and some people try to prove this. Why do you think this is? Would it prove that we have a soul?

Many Christians believe it is the spirit that will live on after death. Christians believe that there will be a Judgement Day and that on this day the bodies of the dead will rise and be made 'perfect' again. The bodies and the spirits of believers will go to heaven.

## ● THE SOUL IN ISLAM

Muslims believe that human beings are **Allah's** highest creation because they are the only living things to have a soul. They believe that Allah gives each human an individual soul soon after the baby begins to develop in the mother's womb. It is this spiritual soul that is the 'real' person. The body is simply a 'carrier'. Allah allows each soul a certain amount of time to inhabit the body.

Muslims believe that life is a test and an opportunity to do good. They believe that good acts will be rewarded in the afterlife by the soul joining Allah in paradise, but evil acts will be punished.

When a Muslim dies, their soul is judged on what they have done in their life and how well they have followed Allah's guidance, for example, if they have asked for forgiveness of sins and followed Muslim duties such as prayer, pilgrimage and helping others.

🎧 **Muslims believe that their soul will join Allah in paradise when they die.**

## THINK ABOUT IT!

2. Think about Muslim and Christian ideas about the soul. For each religion, write down:
   **a)** how these ideas about the soul might affect the ways believers live their lives
   **b)** how believers might behave towards others
   **c)** how believers might feel about death.
   Write at least three sentences for each response.

3. 'You have to believe in God to believe in the existence of the soul!'
   **a)** Do you agree or disagree with this statement? Is the soul something that God gives to humans, or do you think that people have a soul whether they believe in God or not? Think about the arguments behind your answer to this: what is your opinion and why?
   **b)** Some people who are not religious still believe that they have a soul. Why do you think they believe this?

4. Is it the soul that makes human beings unique? Using the ideas you have considered in this lesson, discuss this with a partner and be prepared to feed back to the class. What if you do not believe humans have a soul anyway? Are humans unique at all?

### KEY WORDS

**Spiritual** a way to describe the inner part of a a person, often connected to feelings

**Allah** the Arabic name for God in Islam

In this lesson you will:
- identify Buddhist beliefs about the soul
- reflect on how these beliefs affect the ways Buddhists lead their lives.

**KEY WORDS**

**Samsara** the cycle of life: birth, illness, ageing, death and rebirth

**Reborn** the belief that after death a person's soul moves into another body and continues to live

**Nirvana** point at which Enlightenment has been achieved

**Karma** a teaching that states all actions will influence the next life

Have you ever had the feeling that you have been somewhere before even though you know you have never visited that place? Many scientists think that these feelings, called déjà vu, are simply the result of the mind playing tricks on us. However, some people believe them to be memories of a 'past life'. In other words, you are remembering things that happened to you, or places you have visited, in a life that was previous to the one you are living now.

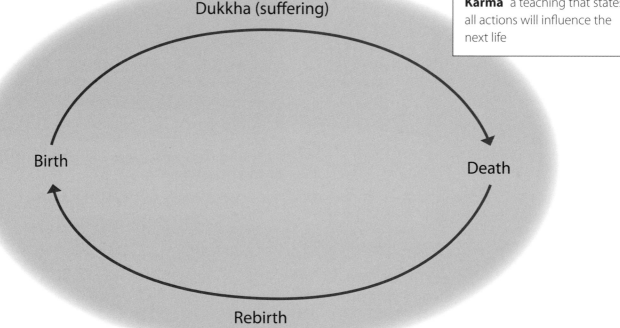

**Buddhists believe in the life cycle of Samsara.**

Buddhists believe that after people die, they will be **reborn** This cycle of birth, illness, ageing, death and rebirth is called Samsara and continues until **Nirvana** is achieved. Buddhists believe that Nirvana is a state of eternal peace (see chapter 4, pages 70–1).

Buddhists also believe that the way they lead their lives will affect their personalities in present and future lives. So, if they deliberately cause harm to others, there will be consequences in their own lives. This idea of consequence is called the law of **karma** (see pages 70–1).

**THINK ABOUT IT!**

1. How might a belief in karma affect the way Buddhists lead their lives?

## ● BUDDHISTS AND THE SOUL

Unlike some other religions such as Christianity, Islam and Judaism, Buddhists do not believe in a God. Nor do they believe that people have an eternal soul. Buddhists believe the idea of a soul is an illusion created by humans who are trying to understand what happens when they die.

However this does not mean that they believe death is the end. Buddhists believe that parts of their personalities and experiences are passed on from one life to the next. So the new life is not exactly the same as the old one, but it has part of the last life within it. Buddhists believe that once we die, the energy of our life force and mind leaves our body. Many Buddhists believe that our life source will then see many visions, some beautiful and some terrifying, depending on how we led our life according to the laws of karma. Eventually, our life force will become reborn as a new creature. If we lived well, according to the law of karma, we will be reborn in a better state, but if we lived badly we will be reborn in a worse state, perhaps even as an animal.

This means Buddhists believe that as part of their make-up, they have memories of past lives and experiences. Some people think that this explains why they have incredibly vivid (realistic) dreams about past lives. In fact there are cases where children as young as two have had their dreams researched by scientists, who have discovered amazing similarities between the child's dream and true people, places and events from the past. Many Buddhists also believe that their personalities partly come from previous lives. Belief in the concept of karma means that their personalities will be especially affected by how good or badly they behaved in past lives.

 **There are 500 million Buddhists in the world. Famous people who are Buddhists include film stars Penelope Cruz , Richard Gere and Keanu Reeves. Why do you think so many people have chosen to become Buddhists today?**

### THINK ABOUT IT!

**2.** Think of your own symbolic example of Buddhist ideas about rebirth and the soul. You can express this as either a short story, like the candle idea, on page 70, or in pictures. Think back to your work on code breaking – your idea must represent Buddhist teachings.

**3.** What do you think of the idea that you have had previous lives?

**4.** Some Buddhists believe that people can be reborn as animals when they are reincarnated. What do you think about this idea? Does it suggest that humans are not unique or different from animals after all?

Consider whether or not the answer to this depends on why a person might be reborn as an animal and not a human – does this make a difference to your thinking? Discuss this with a partner and write a statement of response between you.

**5. a)** What do you think about the idea that we are reborn but God has nothing to do with it?

**b)** If there is no God, who made up the laws of karma?

Discuss these ideas with a partner and write down some of your ideas in a paragraph.

In this lesson you will:
- ask questions about Christian beliefs about creation
- reflect upon how these beliefs might affect the lives of Christians
- evaluate how these beliefs could help Christians to understand what it means to be human.

**THINK ABOUT IT!**

1. How do you think we got here? Who was the first human? You may have heard the expression, 'Which came first – the chicken or the egg?' How would you answer?

> Who came first? You or me?

> What are you asking me for?!

Science has tried to answer the question 'where do we come from?', and it was in response to this that Charles Darwin (1809–82) first proposed his 'theory of evolution'. Darwin suggested that humans have evolved or changed over millions of years, beginning as very simple life forms and becoming more complex as time has moved on – even changing at times to adapt to particular environments. However, many religious people would disagree with this.

## CHRISTIAN CREATION STORIES

The Christian Bible is made up of many different books. The first of these is called Genesis. It is in Genesis that the Christian creation story can be found. The creation story tells of how God created everything that is on the earth and in the heavens. After completing this in six days, God rested on the seventh, having made all kinds of living creatures, including Adam and Eve, the first humans. Some people might find this difficult to believe – how could something as big and complex as the world have been made in just six days? However, if a person is a Christian, do you think this means that they have to read this story 'literally'?

Some Christians believe the creation story is a code or a symbol that has a hidden meaning and represents something else. In this way, they believe that the creation story is a very special story but they might also agree with Darwin's theory.

⤵ **Some Christians believe that the creation story is symbolic. Why? What does this mean?**

## THINK ABOUT IT!

2. Read the creation story in Genesis 1—2: 30. What do you think the creation story in Genesis is telling Christians? What could the hidden meaning be?

**KEY WORDS**

**Symbolic** a representation of an idea or belief

Some Christians think that the creation story tells them more than just how humans were made, but also why they are here. They believe that the story contains hidden meanings about existence and also about the human relationship with God.

Look at the following extracts from Genesis. These quotations have hidden meanings. They can teach Christians about their beliefs in God and also explain why human beings exist and how they should treat the world. Think about what each quotation could mean for Christians.

1) 'You are free to eat from any tree in the garden.' (Genesis 2: 16)

2) 'You must not eat from the tree of the knowledge of good and evil.' (Genesis 2: 17)

3) 'Let us make man in our image, in our likeness, and let them rule ... over all the earth.' (Genesis 1: 26)

4) 'Fill the earth.' (Genesis 1: 28)

## THINK ABOUT IT!

3. Try and match each quotation opposite with one of the following teachings:
   a) obey God and do as He wishes
   b) have a family
   c) enjoy and make the most of the world
   d) have power over the earth but be responsible and look after it.

4. There are many teachings contained within the creation story. Pick out five that you think are most important and explain your choices. Do you think that they are good teachings to follow, even if you are not a Christian?

## ● WHAT DOES THE CREATION STORY TEACH ABOUT HUMANS?

The creation story in Genesis also tells Christians that humanity is different from the rest of creation and other living creatures. In this way, it can explain to Christians what it means to be human. Genesis says that human beings have been made 'in the image of God'. What do you think that this would mean to a Christian?

Think about the ideas you have looked at concerning the soul. Many Christians believe that the soul is a reflection of the image of God inside every person. If animals do not have souls Christians believe that this means that human beings are very special as they can have a relationship with God. How can you link this to what it means to be a human being? Why and how are humans different to other animals?

## THINK ABOUT IT!

5. 'The creation story need not affect the way Christians lead their lives.' Do you agree or disagree with this statement? Give reasons for your answer.

6. What do you think the creation story tells Christians about what it means to be human? Try to link this to what you have learned and make as many points as possible.

In this lesson you will:
- explore what 'ultimate questions' are
- reflect on how ultimate questions can be answered and if they can be answered at all
- evaluate if there is any need to ask ultimate questions and the effect that ultimate questions have on what it means to be human.

🎧 **Where does the universe stop?**

Have you ever laid in bed at night and been kept awake by questions that you just cannot answer – such as:

> Where does space end?

> Are ghosts real? Is there any evidence for them?

> Where does the universe stop?

> What happens to our loved ones when they die?

## ● HOW WOULD YOU RESPOND TO THESE QUESTIONS?

Ultimate questions often cannot be answered. The reason for this is that we do not have the evidence required by science and logic to give us proof. Some people do not need 'proof' – they have faith instead, like a faith in God or an ultimate reality.

The need to answer ultimate questions is often seen as something that makes humanity unique from the rest of creation. Human beings have a conscience and an intellect that often make us crave answers and try to solve life's mysteries.

## THINK ABOUT IT!

1. Having read the ultimate questions on page 102 think of five of your own.

2. **a)** Now with a partner, swap questions and try to answer each others.
   **b)** You may well not be able to answer them – if not, why not?
   **c)** How might you go about trying to find answers?
   **d)** Do you feel as though you actually need to answer them? Why?

Philosophers often try to answer the questions that science cannot help us with. They do this by constructing arguments and thinking carefully about issues that can be confusing. Below are some examples of the arguments that philosophers have used to answer a complicated question: if evil things happen, how can God exist?

'Evil things happen because God has given us free will and we can do as we please.'
*St Augustine (354–430)*

'Evil things happen because God wants us to choose the right thing to do, to show God that we are good people.'
*Irenaeus (c.130–202 CE)*

'We should just have faith in God because that is the point of being religious; we should not need proof as faith does not require proof.'
*Kierkegaard (1813–55)*

## THINK ABOUT IT!

3. **a)** Do you agree with any of the philosophers' responses? Give reasons for your answer.
   **b)** Swap your answer with a partner and read each other's ideas.
   - How do your opinions compare?
   - Has your partner explained their opinions and said why they have come to that conclusion?
   - What could you both do to make your answers even better?

4. 'Asking ultimate questions is pointless because no one can ever really know the answers!' Think about this statement and write a response including as many different views as you can.

In this lesson you will:
- identify prehistoric beliefs about God and the afterlife
- speculate about the meaning of ancient burial practices
- evaluate the idea that humans are unique because they ask 'ultimate questions'.

Some people think that humans are the only 'species' to think about God? Indeed, many religious people believe it is this desire to ask 'ultimate questions', such as 'is there a God?' and 'what happens when we die?' that makes humans unique among all the animals that have ever lived on the earth. But what if humans were not the only animals to ask these questions? What if there were once other species of human-like creatures that asked questions? How would this affect the way that humans think about themselves and about God?

**KEY WORDS**

**Neanderthal** a species of ancient human ancestor related to modern humans

## ● LIFE BEFORE HUMAN BEINGS

Many archaeologists believe that modern humans are not the first species to ask ultimate questions and claim they have discovered evidence to prove this.

Between 1953 and 1960, archaeologists discovered nine human-like skeletons in a cave in Shanidar, Northern Iraq. These were not modern human skeletons, but those of **Neanderthals**.

You might have an image of Neanderthals in your head. They often feature in cartoons as 'prehistoric cave people', wearing animal skin and brandishing a club. Actually, Neanderthals are believed to have been a highly intelligent species of human-like people, living between 250,000 and 30,000 years ago (emerging some 50,000 years before modern humans).

The skeletons discovered at Shanidar were buried 'on purpose'. This alone suggests that Neanderthals thought about things such as 'what happens when we die?' But, even more interestingly, one of the skeletons was discovered with the remains of flowers. Many archaeologists believe that this indicates the body was buried with a garland of flowers placed around its head.

⊃ **This is what a Neanderthal woman would have looked like. Is it what you expected?**

## THINK ABOUT IT!

1. Why do you think this body might have been buried deliberately?

2. Why do you think Neanderthals might have buried their dead with flowers? What might flowers symbolize?

There are many other deliberate Neanderthal burial sites all around Europe and Asia. Another example comes from Dolni Vestonice in the Czech Republic in 1986. A group of three skeletons was discovered. These appear to have been buried beneath burnt wood. Many artefacts were placed around the bodies such as seashell and snail shell decorations, animal teeth and red paint.

In archaeology, nobody ever really knows what happened because nobody alive today actually saw what happened. All people can do is 'interpret'. They make educated and intelligent suggestions based on the evidence.

How would you interpret these burials? What do you think happened? What might these artefacts and practices symbolize?

◗ **This is the archaeological site of the Dolni Vestonice burial. Over 27,000 years passed between burial and discovery.**

**?**

## THINK ABOUT IT!

3. Look at the diagram of the Dolni Vestonice burial site. For each of the artefacts, try to come up with an interpretation of what it might symbolize. Give reasons for your answers.

4. 'If humans are not the first and only animals to ask ultimate questions such as "what happens when we die?" and "is there a God?" religious people are wrong to think that humans are unique and special.' Do you agree or disagree with this statement? Give reasons for your answer and try to include more than one point of view.

In this lesson you will:
- investigate what human rights are
- reflect on the need for human rights in the world today
- evaluate whether all people in the world have human rights today.

## THE UNIVERSAL DECLARATION OF HUMAN RIGHTS

During the Second World War (1939–45) over fifty million people were killed. Six million of these were Jews who died as a result of persecution by the Nazis.

After the First World War (1914–18), many Germans believed the Jews were to blame for Germany's economic problems. The Nazis wanted to capture every Jew in Europe, with the aim of destroying the Jewish race. To do this, they built concentration camps, where they would be worked to death or executed. This event in history is called the Holocaust or the **Shoah**. The deliberate killing of a very large number of people from a particular ethnic group or nation is called 'genocide'.

When the world discovered the atrocities committed by the Nazis, 51 countries, including Britain and the United States of America, joined an organization called the United Nations with the aim of never allowing genocide to happen again. They created an agreement of the basic rights of every human being in the world. This is called the Universal Declaration of Human Rights and is very important today.

🎧 **What do you think is happening to these children?**

**?**

### THINK ABOUT IT!

1. What other basic human rights would you add to this list? Try to think of at least five.

**An example of five human rights**

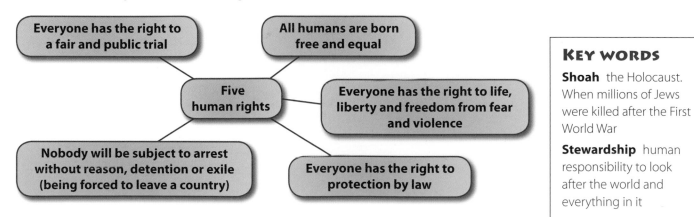

- Everyone has the right to a fair and public trial
- All humans are born free and equal
- Five human rights
- Everyone has the right to life, liberty and freedom from fear and violence
- Nobody will be subject to arrest without reason, detention or exile (being forced to leave a country)
- Everyone has the right to protection by law

### KEY WORDS

**Shoah** the Holocaust. When millions of Jews were killed after the First World War

**Stewardship** human responsibility to look after the world and everything in it

## ● WHO IS RESPONSIBLE FOR PROTECTING HUMAN RIGHTS?

Many people believe that this entitlement to human rights, and responsibility for the protection of the human rights of others, is one of the things that sets humans apart from other forms of life. They believe humans have a responsibility to look after the world, its people and animals. This responsibility is often called **stewardship**.

> ❛When an alien lives with you in your land, do not ill-treat him. The alien living with you must be treated as one of your native-born. Love him as yourself, for you were aliens in Egypt. I am the LORD your God.❜
>
> *From the third book of the Hebrew Bible (Leviticus 19:33–34)*

## ● HOW SUCCESSFUL IS THE UNIVERSAL DECLARATION OF HUMAN RIGHTS?

- In the world today there are estimated to be over 300,000 child soldiers, with the youngest being seven years old.

- Over 40 million children live homeless on the streets of the world's cities. To put this into perspective, the UK has a population of 60 million.

- Children are regularly executed in 34 countries.

- 2800 children were murdered in Colombia in 1991 during a bitter civil war. By 1993 the number had risen to over 2900, an average of 6 per day.

- Over the last hundred years, 100 million people have died as a result of war, famine and abuse.

How do these statistics make you feel? Shocked? Horrified? Lucky? Millions of people are being exploited and abused in every country on the planet, every single day. So, how successful is the Universal Declaration of Human Rights?

**There are more than 300,000 children forced to be soldiers in the world today.**

### THINK ABOUT IT!

2. 'You don't have to be religious to care about human rights'. Discuss in pairs then share your ideas as a class.

### THINK ABOUT IT!

3. What things are happening in the world today that break basic human rights? Think about things you have heard about in the news recently.

4. 'If you see it as necessary to murder people, can they please be murdered where I do not need to see it?' A woman who lived near to Auschwitz (a concentration camp in Poland) wrote this to the Nazi government during the Second World War. Think about what you know about the Holocaust and your own views on human rights. How would you react if you knew that genocide was happening on your doorstep? Explain your answer.

## WHAT THIS TASK IS ALL ABOUT:

**1** Why do some religious people, and non-believers, think that humans are unique (different from every other animal) in the world?

**2** Do humans 'deserve' to be, as some people believe, so special?

## WHAT YOU NEED TO DO TO COMPLETE THE TASK:

**1** For question 1, you need to describe some of the following beliefs and ideas: ultimate questions, beliefs about life after death, beliefs about the soul, human rights and the Christian creation story in Genesis. You may also wish to explore the idea that we may not be unique by explaining Neanderthal burial rituals.

**2** For question 2, you need to explain and evaluate arguments for and against the idea that humans deserve to be special. To do this, you may wish to talk about ideas such as stewardship, religious beliefs about life after death, the soul, and good and bad things that humans have done in the world (try to give some examples). Complete your answer with a conclusion, explaining what you think.

## HINTS AND TIPS

**1** For question 1, look back at some of the key ideas that you have looked at in this chapter. You may wish to focus especially on religious ideas about creation and Christian, Muslim and Buddhist beliefs about the soul.

**2** For question 2, you may wish to focus especially on human rights. Remember to give a balanced view and explain your own ideas about whether humans deserve to be special.

## TO ACHIEVE   YOU WILL NEED TO

**Level 3**

Give a basic description of one or two of the ideas that you have looked at.

**Level 4**

Give a detailed description of a few of the ideas that you have looked at and a basic explanation of these ideas.

**Level 5**

Give detailed descriptions and explanations of a range of ideas explored in this chapter.

**Level 6**

Give detailed descriptions and explanations of a range of ideas explored in this chapter. For question 2, you will need to evaluate arguments for and against humans deserving to be 'special'.

# GLOSSARY

**Aboriginal** the first, native people of Australia

**Agnostic** someone who is unsure whether God exists or not

**Ahimsa** non violence, respect for life

**Akirah** Islamic belief in life after death

**Allah** the Arabic name for God in Islam

**Archbishop** one of the most important leaders in Christianity

**Atheist** someone who does not believe in the existence of a God

**Authority** the power or right to be a leader of others

**Belief** something that you feel is true, but you cannot prove

**Bishop** a Christian leader

**Brahman** the supreme God in Hinduism, understood to be ultimate reality

**Calligraphy** the fine art of handwriting

**Charisma** a special quality that makes a person different and inspiring

**Code** a system of letters or symbols which express a hidden meaning

**Conscience** how people decide what is right or wrong

**Creator** the person who brings something into existence

**Cultures** the different beliefs and practices of societies

**Deities** gods and goddesses in Hinduism

**Disciplined** controlled behaviour that follows rules

**Divine** being holy or sacred

**Dreamtime** the creation of the world as described in the sacred stories of the Australian Aborigines

**Epic** a long story or poem which tells of a famous person or event

**Faith** trust and confidence in something or someone

**Five Precepts** five moral intentions that Buddhists try to live their life by

**Gospel** the first four books of the New Testament: Matthew, Mark, Luke and John

**Granthi** reader of the Guru Granth Sahib who leads ceremonies in Sikhism

**Gurdwara** a Sikh place of worship

**Gurmukh** someone who lives by the Gurus' teaching

**Guru** a religious teacher in Hinduism and Sikhism

**Guru Granth Sahib** the holy book of Sikhism

**Hadiths** saying and traditions of Muhammad

**Holy** devoted to God

**Humanist** someone who believes that all values should be based on human experience and reason

**Ik Onkar** religious symbol in Sikhism expressing belief in one God

**Image** a visual way of expressing an idea

**Imam** a leader of prayer in Islam

**Interpretation** giving a meaning for something

**Karma** a teaching that states all actions will influence the next life

**Kirpan** one of the five K's, a sword

**Kosher** food seen as pure and acceptable by Jews according to the Torah

**Langar** the kitchen and dining hall in a gurdwara and the food served in it

**Leadership** the role of leading a person or a group

**Mandala** circular pattern used in worship and meditation

**Meditate** to calm the mind in order to concentrate or pray

**Meditation** calming the mind by concentrating

**Mitzvot** Jewish religious laws, good deeds or duties

**Monotheistic** belief in only one God

**Mool Mantar** statement of belief at the beginning of the Guru Granth Sahib

**Moral** the correct way to behave

**Moral code** a set of rules that help people decide the right thing to do

**Mukti** the escape from rebirth

**Murti** figures which represent gods and goddesses in Hinduism

**Myth** a story told to express beliefs about God or the world

**Narrative** a spoken or written way of expressing ideas

**Neanderthal** a species of ancient human ancestor related to modern humans

**Nirvana** point at which Enlightenment has been achieved

**Omnipotent** the belief that God has unlimited power

**Omnipresent** the belief that God is in all places at the same time

**Omniscient** the belief that God knows everything that is going on in the world

**Philosophers** great thinkers who try to understand the meaning of life

**Pope** the head of the Roman Catholic Church

**Protestant** a part of the Christian Church different from the Roman Catholic and Orthodox churches

**Puja** Hindu act of worship to show devotion to God

**Qur'an** the holy book of Islam

**Reincarnation** the belief that after death a person's soul moves into another body and continues to live

**Representation** a way of showing something

**Responsibility** looking after, managing, taking the blame on behalf of others

**Resurrection** the belief that Jesus rose from the dead after his crucifixion. It can also mean a new life for Christians

**Ritual** an action, or series of actions, that follow a certain pattern

**Sacred** another word for God or the divine

**Sacred** dedicated to God or a religious purpose

**Samsara** the cycle of life: birth, illness, ageing, death and rebirth

**Sawm** Islamic practice of fasting from sunrise to sunset

**Scholars** great thinkers who have developed our understanding

**Sewa** Sikh requirement to help others

**Shahadah** Islamic declaration of faith in Allah

**Shema** a prayer used by Jews maintaining belief in one God

**Shoah** the Holocaust. When millions of Jews were killed after the First World War

**Soul** the non-physical, spiritual or emotional centre of a person that is said to survive death

**Spirit** the inner part of a person, often connected to feelings

**Shabbat** Jewish name for the holy day also known as the Sabbath

**Stewardship** human responsibility to look after the world and everything in it

**Story** spoken or written account which expresses ideas through description

**Symbol** something which is used to represent something else

**Symbolic** a representation of an idea or belief

**Symmetrical** having a pattern with equal and matching shapes

**Synagogue** Jewish place of worship

**Tawhid** belief in the oneness of Allah

**Theist** someone who believes in the existence of a God or Gods

**Torah** Jewish Books of the Law, the first five books of the Tenakh

**Trimurti** the three gods of creation, sustaining and destruction - Brahma, Vishnu and Shiva

**Trinity** the Christian belief that there are three persons within one God: the Father, the Son and the Holy Spirit

**Unity** the state of being harmonious and united

**Vicar** a Christian leader in charge of worship in a parish

**Vocation** a job, or way of living, that reflects a person's religious beliefs

**Zakah** Islamic practise of giving 2.5 per cent of savings to those in need

# INDEX